Table of Contents

Take Charge of Your Cognitive Health

· ·

Your brain, like your body, needs care and maintenance to stay fit and functioning.

Aging—it's a fact of life, like death and taxes. It affects the mind as well as the body. And it starts the moment you're born. But that doesn't mean you have to just sit around waiting for the years to take their mental toll. A growing body of evidence suggests that protecting your noggin and taking other steps to preserve and enhance your brain power along the way may help keep your brain from showing its age.

Pumping new life into your thinking cap is what this book is all about. How do different parts of the brain work? How does food affect your thinking? What exactly is memory? What is the relationship between quality of sleep and cognitive decline? We'll explore these and other topics and provide you with techniques to improve your cognitive functioning.

But first we'll start with a section of timed puzzles to challenge different kinds of cognitive skills. Take the assessment and write down your results. At the end of the book you'll find a second series of timed puzzles. Did your time improve? If you incorporated the practices outlined in this book, you should see improved cognitive skills.

- *The average human brain has over 85 billion neurons.*
- *Estimates of human memory vary from 1 to 1,000 terabytes.*
- *A human brain may have as many as 1,000 trillion synaptic connections.*
- *There are about 400 capillaries in the brain.*
- *Your brain is over 70% water.*
- *The brain consumes around 20-25% of calories burned per day.*
- *There may be 1,000 to 10,000 synapses associated with a single neuron.*
- *Together, your neurons produce enough electricity to power a light bulb.*

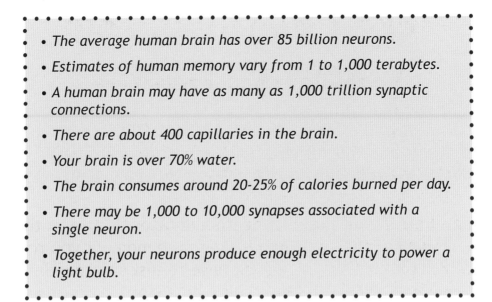

Diet, exercise, sleep, and mental stimulation: the foundations of good cognitive health!

Start Your Engines

Different kinds of puzzles engage different aspects of your brain and different neural pathways. Whenever you sit down for a "cognitive exercise session," change up your puzzle routine with a variety of different types of puzzles. We've made this easy to do with an assessment of 12 very different puzzles to get you started.

Don't be intimidated if you come across types of puzzles that you've never seen and that challenge your mental powers. Instead of avoiding these tough ones, welcome them. To be effective as a mental workout, the puzzles should not be too easy or too difficult. And to be effective as an assessment of your brain age, they should stimulate all your major areas of concentration and cognition!

We'd like you to set a timer for 60 minutes and complete these 12 puzzles to the best of your ability. At the end of this book, you'll find 12 more puzzles to give you another snapshot of your brain age. Before you know it, your puzzle-cracking ability will improve, your confidence will grow, and this will be a source of satisfaction and even pride. You'll be able to see how much you improved both in thinking ability and speed.

SOLVE IT

Solve each problem in your head, then circle the correct answer.

22 + 43 =	55	65	67
8 × 4 × 1 =	32	33	34
103 + 36 =	135	138	139
12 × 8 =	84	94	96
111 ÷ 3 =	37	38	39
73 − 48 =	25	35	36
13 × 7 =	91	101	121
48 ÷ 3 =	12	16	18
4 × 2 × 4 × 2 =	32	64	128
101 − 56 =	35	41	45
21 + 37 =	55	56	58
33 − 18 =	12	13	15
3 × 3 × 3 =	9	18	27
54 ÷ 9 =	6	7	8
84 − 46 =	36	38	44

FIND "NOW"

Ignoring spaces and punctuation, how many occurrences of the consecutive letters N-O-W can you find in the paragraph below? Circle each instance.

During the snowstorm, Howard played Uno with Zowie, not knowing when the snowstorm would end. Unbeknownst to Howard, Zowie had no worries about winning because she knows how to palm Uno cards. Losing badly, Howard had a plan. "Ow!" he yelled, pretending to get a paper cut and sending the cards from Uno whirling to the floor. "Now you've done it," yelled Zowie, and she donned her snowshoes and left, knowing Howard had figured her out.

Answers on page 23.

REMEMBER ME

Look at the pictures for 2 minutes. After 2 minutes, turn the page.

REMEMBER ME

Which objects did you see on page 9? Circle Yes or No next to each object's name.

PIANO	YES	NO
UMBRELLA	YES	NO
FLAG	YES	NO
WINDMILL	YES	NO
BANANAS	YES	NO
GRATER	YES	NO
DOUGHNUTS	YES	NO
BOTTLE	YES	NO
HARMONICA	YES	NO
CAMERA	YES	NO
ANCHOR	YES	NO
VIOLIN	YES	NO
PINEAPPLE	YES	NO
COMPASS	YES	NO
TEAPOT	YES	NO
PUMPKIN	YES	NO

Answers on page 23.

CHANGE IN THE AIR

How fast can you arrange the stacks of coins from smallest to largest in monetary value? Write the letter order in the blanks.

___ ___ ___ ___ ___ ___

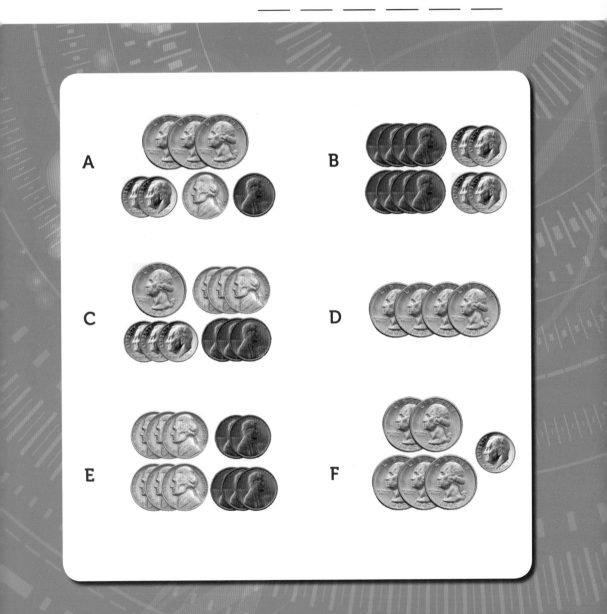

SWIMMING WITH THE CUBES

Which one of the cubes can be made from the unfolded sample at the center? Circle the cube.

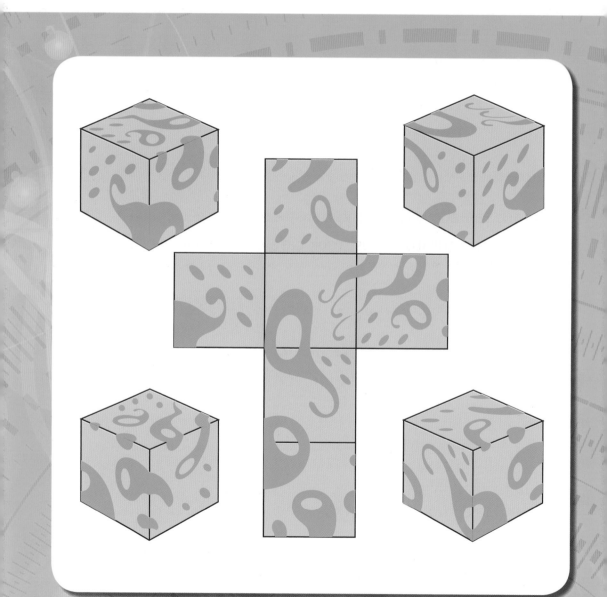

Answer on page 24.

WHAT A WHISTLE

Read the story that follows. Then turn the page for a quiz on what you've read.

When I was 14, I used to hang out at a nature center in Connecticut, where I grew up.

One day a man brought in a sparrow hawk with a busted wing. These days the official name of the bird is the American kestrel, but they will always be sparrow hawks to me. Anyway, it was a little beauty, a small falcon about the size of a jay, with beautiful colors — blue-gray wings, rufous tail and back — and that piercing gaze of hawks.

One of the curators, Les, took care of the sparrow hawk for a few months, feeding it small strips of raw meat. As the bird's wing grew stronger, Les started retraining it to fly indoors, holding a piece of meat in a gloved hand. He'd stand close at first, so the bird could practically jump to his hand, but then he'd stand farther and farther away. Soon the little hawk was flying to him for the food.

Each time Les held out the food, he'd do this remarkable whistle, which he said was the sound of a screech owl. It had a slightly eerie, tremulous sound. You do the whistle by fluttering the back of your tongue loosely against your palate. It's hard to explain. I practiced a lot, and soon I could do it too. People always seem surprised at the sound — it's not a typical whistle. You can vary the pitch to high or low by how you flutter your tongue. I don't have a lot of talents, but by gum I can do the screech-owl whistle!

WHAT A WHISTLE (PART 2)

Circle an answer to each question.

1. In which state did the author grow up?
    COLORADO   CONNETICUT   NEW HAMPSHIRE

2. Another name for the "sparrow hawk" is:
    BLUE GROUSE   AMERICAN KESTREL   PURPLE FINCH

3. How old is the author at the time of the story?
    12   13   14

4. What color are the sparrow hawk's wings?
    BLUE-GRAY   GREENISH   BROWN

5. Sparrow hawks in captivity can be fed:
    CELERY   POTATOES   RAW MEAT

6. The sparrow hawk in the story had:
    A BAD WING   A BROKEN LEG   MISSING TAIL FEATHERS

7. The sparrow hawk is a type of:
    SHORE BIRD   FALCON   JAY

8. As the bird healed, the curator:
    LET IT GO   RETRAINED IT TO FLY   TOOK IT HOME

9. The curator trained the bird by using:
    A CERTAIN WHISTLE   A CLUCKING SOUND   A DUCK DECOY

10. The sound the curator made was that of:
    A BALD EAGLE   A SCREECH OWL   A BARN OWL

Answers on page 24.

BOOKEND LETTERS

Each word below is missing a pair of identical letters. Add the same letter to the beginning and end of each word to create new words. Do not use any pair of letters twice.

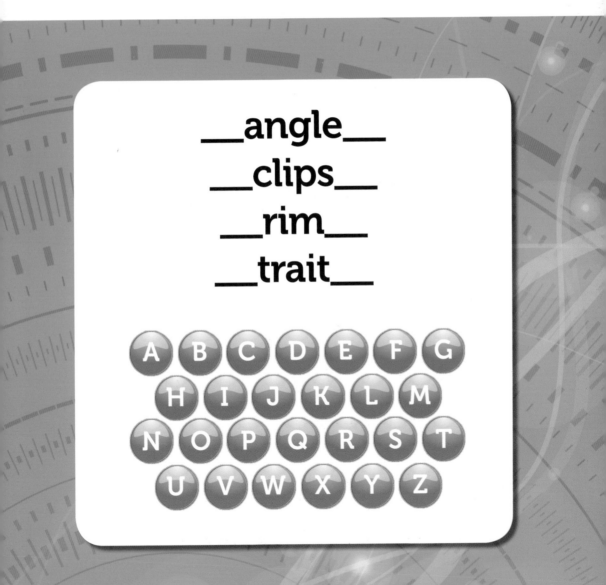

__angle__

__clips__

__rim__

__trait__

A B C D E F G
H I J K L M
N O P Q R S T
U V W X Y Z

Answers on page 24.

SCHOOL SUPPLIES

How many dots can you find in the picture below? Circle the answer.

108 112 114 115 116

Answer on page 24.

W-CUBED RECTANGLES

Which of the shapes below can be folded to form the cube at the center? There may be more than one. Circle your selections(s).

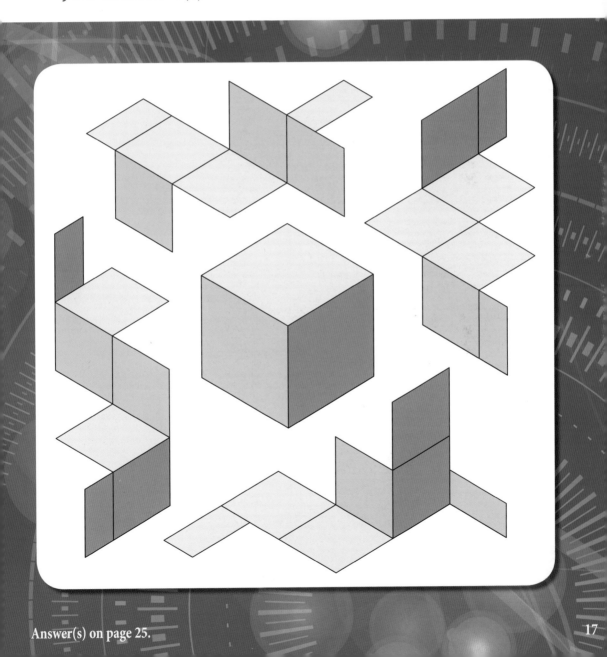

Answer(s) on page 25.

MISSING SIGNS

For each equation, one sign will complete both sides of the equation. Fill in the boxes.

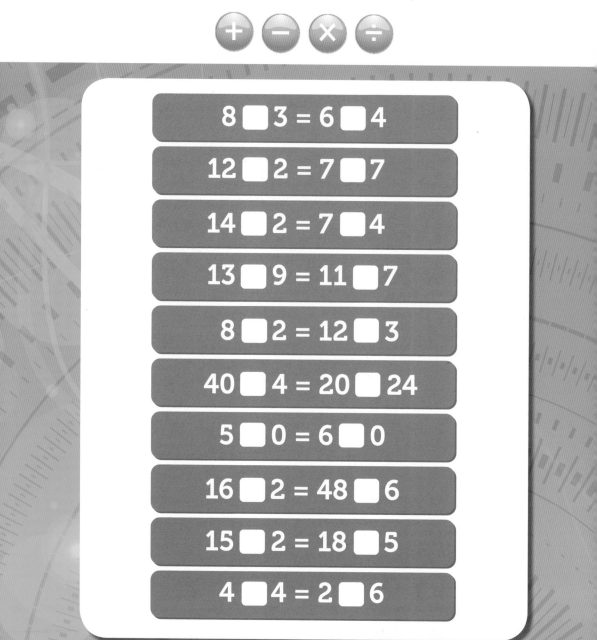

8 ☐ 3 = 6 ☐ 4

12 ☐ 2 = 7 ☐ 7

14 ☐ 2 = 7 ☐ 4

13 ☐ 9 = 11 ☐ 7

8 ☐ 2 = 12 ☐ 3

40 ☐ 4 = 20 ☐ 24

5 ☐ 0 = 6 ☐ 0

16 ☐ 2 = 48 ☐ 6

15 ☐ 2 = 18 ☐ 5

4 ☐ 4 = 2 ☐ 6

Answers on page 25.

MEMORY MISHMASH

Look at the shapes for 2 minutes, then turn the page.

MEMORY MISHMASH

1. How many white triangles are found in the grid?

   a) 1
   b) 2
   c) 3

2. Which shape is found to the right of the black triangle?

   a) heart
   b) sun
   c) infinity sign

3. Which shape is found above the sun shape?

   a) white triangle
   b) white circle
   c) white square

4. Which shape is found in two contiguous spaces?

   a) white triangle
   b) white circle
   c) white square

5. How many white circles are found in the grid?

   a) 1
   b) 2
   c) 3

6. Which shape is found in the top left corner of the grid?

   a) white triangle
   b) heart
   c) infinity sign

7. Which shape is found in the lowest right corner of the grid?

   a) white triangle
   b) white square
   c) infinity sign

8. Which shape is found above the infinity sign?

   a) white circle
   b) white square
   c) white triangle

Answers on page 25.

PATTERN MEMORIZATION

Look at the shapes for 2 minutes. After 2 minutes, turn the page.

PATTERN MEMORIZATION

What shapes complete the pattern? Fill in the spaces.

Answer on page 25.

ANSWERS

SOLVE IT (pg. 7)

22 + 43 = ~~55~~ **65** ~~57~~

8 × 4 × 1 = **32** ~~33~~ ~~34~~

103 + 36 = ~~135~~ ~~138~~ **139**

12 × 8 = ~~84~~ ~~94~~ **96**

111 ÷ 3 = **37** ~~38~~ ~~39~~

73 − 48 = **25** ~~35~~ ~~36~~

13 × 7 = **91** ~~101~~ ~~121~~

48 ÷ 3 = ~~12~~ **16** ~~18~~

4 × 2 × 4 × 2 = ~~32~~ **64** ~~128~~

101 − 56 = ~~35~~ ~~41~~ **45**

21 + 37 = ~~35~~ ~~56~~ **58**

33 − 18 = ~~12~~ ~~13~~ **15**

3 × 3 × 3 = ~~9~~ ~~18~~ **27**

54 ÷ 9 = **6** ~~7~~ ~~8~~

84 − 46 = ~~36~~ **38** ~~44~~

REMEMBER ME (pg. 9–10)

PIANO — No
UMBRELLA — Yes
FLAG — Yes
WINDMILL — No
BANANAS — No
GRATER — Yes
DOUGHNUTS — Yes
BOTTLE — No
HARMONICA — Yes
CAMERA — No
ANCHOR — Yes
VIOLIN — No
PINEAPPLE — Yes
COMPASS — Yes
TEAPOT — No
PUMPKIN — No

FIND "NOW" (pg. 8)   (12)

During the snowstorm, Howard played Uno with Zowie, not knowing when the snowstorm would end. Unbeknownst to Howard, Zowie had no worries about winning because she knows how to palm Uno cards. Losing badly, Howard had a plan. "Ow!" he yelled, pretending to get a paper cut and sending the cards from Uno whirling to the floor. "Now you've done it," yelled Zowie, and she donned her snowshoes and left, knowing Howard had figured her out.

CHANGE IN THE AIR (pg. 11)

E B C D A F

SWIMMING WITH THE CUBES (pg. 12)

The bottom left cube matches the sample.

BOOKEND LETTERS (pg. 15)

Dangle**D**

Eclips**E**

Prim**P**

Strait**S**

SCHOOL SUPPLIES (pg. 16)

WHAT A WHISTLE (pg. 13–14)

1. CONNECTICUT
2. AMERICAN KESTREL
3. 14
4. BLUE-GRAY
5. RAW MEAT
6. A BAD WING
7. FALCON
8. RETRAINED IT TO FLY
9. A CERTAIN WHISTLE
10. A SCREECH OWL

W-CUBED RECTANGLES (pg. 17)

The bottom two shapes can be folded to form the cube.

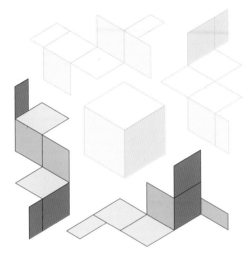

MISSING SIGNS (pg. 18)

8 x 3 = 6 x 4

12 + 2 = 7 + 7

14 x 2 = 7 x 4

13 − 9 = 11 − 7

8 ÷ 2 = 12 ÷ 3

40 + 4 = 20 + 24

5 x 0 = 6 x 0

16 ÷ 2 = 48 ÷ 6

15 − 2 = 18 − 5

4 + 4 = 2 + 6

MEMORY MISHMASH (pg. 19-20)

1. b) 2

2. a) heart

3. a) white triangle

4. c) white square

5. a) 1

6. a) white triangle

7. c) infinity sign

8. a) white circle

PATTERN MEMORIZATION (pg. 21-22)

The Amazing Brain

No other organ in the body—and no computer in existence—is as complex as the human brain. It governs the functions and actions of the body and is the wellspring of complex thought, self-awareness, feelings, memories, insights, and personality. It's what makes us uniquely human and what makes each of us humans truly unique.

While there is still much we do not know about the brain, our understanding of its anatomy and functioning has advanced more in the last 25 years than in all of previous history. Much of that insight has come as the result of new brain-imaging technologies. These windows into the brain have helped scientists identify many of the brain's capabilities in memory, reasoning, and creative thought.

Looking Inward

Much of our current understanding of how the brain works has come through the use of two medical imaging technologies—functional magnetic resonance imaging (fMRI) and positron emission tomography (PET) scans. They've given us the unique ability to visualize the brain in action without cutting into the skull.

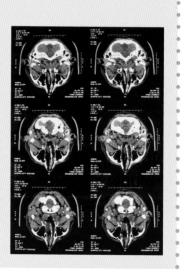

Both fMRI and PET scans work on the theory that blood flow increases in areas of the brain that are currently

most engaged, because cells that are hard at work need more oxygen and glucose, or blood sugar, to fuel their increased activity.

In fMRI, a strong magnetic field is used to identify the parts of the brain that are using the most oxygen. In a PET scan, a trace amount of radioactive glucose is injected into the bloodstream, and the brain cells that are working hardest take up more of the glucose. In both cases, a computer then generates an image in which the most active brain areas appear highlighted in bright colors (with the color red indicating the sections of most intense activity).

We now know that while the various parts of the brain work together, each seems to have its areas of expertise. The hindbrain, which consists of the upper part of the spinal cord, the lower portion of the brain stem, and the cerebellum, is in charge of essential, automatic body functions, such as heartbeat, blood pressure, and breathing. The cerebellum, a wrinkly round clump at the lower back end of the brain, also controls and coordinates voluntary movements, balance, and posture; it helps to keep you upright as you walk; and it kicks in when you perform an action that you've learned by heart, such as a dance step or a baseball swing.

The uppermost portion of the brain stem, referred to as the midbrain, has a variety of functions, including control of reflex actions involving vision and hearing. So when something catches your attention, it's the midbrain that prompts your eyes to move in the direction of the object and your head to tilt toward the sound to better identify the source.

Sitting above the hindbrain and midbrain is the forebrain, the largest part of the human brain. It consists of the cerebrum, or topmost portion of the brain, and important structures that lie deep within the brain, such as the thalamus and hypothalamus.

The thalamus, which acts as the relay station for incoming signals from the rest of the body, conveys sensations of pain, touch, temperature, and the like to the rest of the brain for processing. Surrounding the thalamus is the hypothalamus, and attached to the hypothalamus by a thin stalk is the pituitary gland. Because the pituitary controls most of the hormones in the body, the hypothalamus is thought to have a major influence on hormone-regulated drives such as hunger, thirst, and sexual desire.

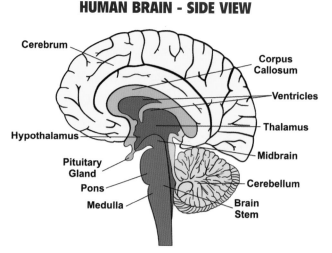

HUMAN BRAIN - SIDE VIEW

Cerebrum
Corpus Callosum
Ventricles
Thalamus
Hypothalamus
Midbrain
Pituitary Gland
Pons
Cerebellum
Medulla
Brain Stem

But the cerebrum is the part of the brain that we're most interested in here. The cerebrum is relatively larger in humans than in other animals, making up roughly 85 percent of a human's brain weight. And it's the part of the brain that distinguishes us from all other living creatures on the planet. It makes us far better problem solvers and decision makers. It allows us to think about something that occurred in the past and imagine and plan for what may happen in the future. It not only enables us to learn but gives us the ability to analyze how we learn. And it is the source of both our intelligence and our ability to appreciate that intelligence.

The cerebrum's thin, gray, convoluted outer layer is called the cerebral cortex. This surface layer, with its rounded folds of tissue and deep grooves, is what typically comes to mind when we picture what the brain actually looks like. Its gray color comes from the nerve cells in this layer of tissue. Unlike most of the other nerve cells in the brain, which appear white because they have a protective coating of insulation, the ones in the cerebral cortex lack insulation. But that doesn't mean they're not important. Indeed, the majority of the brain's information processing goes on in the cerebral cortex. And scientists suspect that all those folds and grooves are there to increase the brain's surface area, allowing far more of this highly active gray matter to fit within the confines of the skull than would be possible if the cerebral cortex were stretched out smooth.

The cerebrum is divided into two halves, or hemispheres, by a deep fissure. These two halves are often referred to as the right and left sides of the brain. Despite being separated, the two hemispheres constantly communicate via a thick band of nerve fibers called the corpus callosum, which is located at the bottom of the fissure. The nerve fibers that lead out of the two hemispheres, toward the body, actually cross

> **The Lightness of Being**
>
> *At birth, a human brain weighs about two-thirds of a pound, but it jumps in size during the first year of life to about two pounds. The brain reaches its maximum weight of roughly three pounds around the age of 20.*

one another in the brain stem before they progress down the spinal cord. As a result, each of these cerebral hemispheres generally controls functions on the opposite side of the body. For example, a region in the left hemisphere of the brain actually controls the movement of the right arm. (No one knows why the brain is designed in this way.)

Each of the cerebral hemispheres, in turn, can be divided into sections referred to as lobes. Each of these lobes controls a different group of functions. Some of those functions are noted below.

Frontal lobes. The lobes that lie immediately behind your forehead, on either side of the fissure, are called the frontal lobes. The frontal lobes are the home of self-awareness and personality. They're the primary seat of reasoning, planning, and problem-solving capabilities, as well. They allow you to hold more than one idea in mind so that you can consider them at the same time and weigh them against one another. They allow you to see patterns in objects, facts, or events and

HUMAN BRAIN ANATOMY

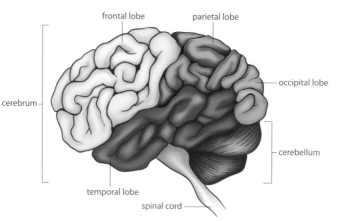

frontal lobe parietal lobe

occipital lobe

cerebrum

cerebellum

temporal lobe

spinal cord

draw wider conclusions from them. They're essential to using language to express thoughts and emotions and to keeping behavior in check. Each frontal lobe also has an area called the primary motor cortex, which controls the body's voluntary movements.

Parietal lobes. Sitting behind the frontal lobes are the parietal lobes, which accept and process input from the body's senses. These lobes are also important for written language skills. It's here that the brain recognizes groups of letters as words and ties words to thoughts. The parietal lobes also allow us to perceive spatial relations and to separate or group things by characteristics such as shape and size.

Occipital lobes. The occipital lobes are situated at the back of the cerebrum, behind the parietal lobes and above the cerebellum. These lobes are all about processing information from the eyes. They allow us to see and to recognize what we're seeing, to perceive color and depth, and to track objects in our visual field.

Temporal lobes. The temporal lobes sit on either side of the cerebrum, near the ears, which provides a clue to one of their major functions. These lobes allow us to perceive and recognize sound. They give us the ability to understand spoken language and appreciate music. The temporal lobes are also vital to regulating emotion, remembering, reasoning, and learning.

Instant Messaging

As the body's control center, the brain receives input from the sensory organs and muscles. It interprets and analyzes that input and sends directions back out to the body. The spinal cord and a complex system of peripheral nerves—which branch out from the brain and spinal cord to the rest of the body—do the work of relaying those messages back and forth. Together, the brain, spinal cord, and peripheral nerves make up the body's nervous system.

The basic building block of the nervous system is the nerve cell, or neuron. The brain is packed with neurons—tens of billions of them. Neurons bundled together by connective tissue run up and down the spinal cord and form the nerves that branch out to the far reaches of the body.

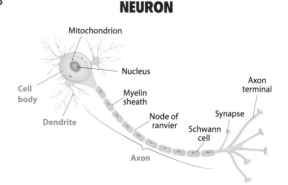

NEURON

Mitochondrion

Nucleus

Cell body

Myelin sheath

Dendrite

Node of ranvier

Axon terminal

Synapse

Schwann cell

Axon

Filled with Glia

Although there are many billions of neurons in the brain and spinal cord, they're not the only cells present. As a matter of fact, there are far more glia, or glial cells, than there are nerve cells in the brain and spinal cord—an estimated 10 to 50 times more. The name glia means "glue," and for a long time, scientists believed that glial cells simply formed a supportive structure, kind of like scaffolding, for neurons. But more recent research has made clear that the various types of glial cells are far more active and do much more than simply hold neurons in place. Glial cells supply neurons with nutrients, sweep up debris, and otherwise help to maintain a healthy environment for nerve cells. Some glia are essential to the so-called blood-brain barrier that helps to keep many potentially harmful substances from entering the brain's blood supply. Other glial cells produce myelin, the fatty substance that wraps around and insulates the axons of most nerve cells, allowing impulses to travel more quickly. And those are just some of the glia functions that scientists have uncovered so far. Research into these busy little cells continues.

But neurons can't speak, write notes, or send texts. They're not even physically connected to one another. So how do they communicate with each other, with muscle cells, and with cells in our eyes, skin, and other sensory organs? They use signals—made not of smoke but of chemicals and electricity. These specialized cells of the nervous system are very sensitive to chemical stimulation, excellent at transmitting electrical impulses, and designed to relay messages.

A Lot of Nerve

If you laid out all of the nerves in an adult human's body, end-to-end, they would stretch for nearly 50 miles.

Each neuron has a cell body, just as other types of cells do. But on one side of this body, the neuron has dendrites, short appendages that stick out like arms and legs. And on the opposite side of the cell body is an arm of varying length called an axon. The axon is usually protected by an insulating sheath made of a fatty substance called myelin, which also helps electrical impulses move more quickly down the axon. At the far end of the axon are tiny sacs capable of releasing a variety of special chemicals known as neurotransmitters.

SYNAPSE

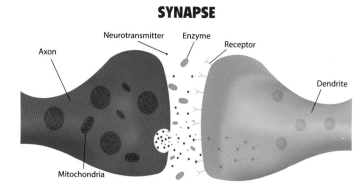

Neurotransmitter   Enzyme

Axon   Receptor

Dendrite

Mitochondria

The Long and Short of It

The length of a nerve cell's axon depends on where the cell is located and how far it is from the other cells it communicates with. The axon of a neuron within the brain tends to be only millimeters in length because the neurons it talks to are all very close together. A neuron that extends from the brain down the spinal cord or from the spinal cord to your foot, on the other hand, is going to have a far longer axon. Some axons in the human body are more than three feet long!

When a nerve cell is stimulated by another nerve cell or by a cell from a muscle or sensory organ, a low-level electrical impulse is generated and speeds down the axon, away from the cell body. When the impulse reaches the far end of the axon, it triggers the release of certain neurotransmitter chemicals from tiny sacs. Those neurotransmitters diffuse across the gap—called a synapse—between that nerve cell's axon and a neighboring nerve cell's dendrites. Receptors on the dendrites of the neighboring nerve cell take up the neurotransmitters. The neurotransmitters stimulate changes in the neighboring nerve cell, which in turn trigger an electrical impulse that races down its axon toward the next synapse, and so on.

In this way, signals from the farthest reaches of the body are relayed to and from the brain and signals pass between nerve cells in the brain itself. As hard as it may be to comprehend, every sensation you experience, every emotion you feel, every movement you make and sound you utter, every memory and thought you have, and everything you "know" is the result of electrical and chemical signals crossing unique patterns of nerve cells and synapses.

An Overnight Sensation

When your foot or arm "falls asleep" because of the way you were sitting or lying down, it happens because pressure has been applied to the body part in such a way that the nerves can't transmit signals from the brain to the body part, and vice versa. The "pins and needles" sensation comes from the nerve waking up.

Learning, Remembering, and Growing

Every experience we have as we go about our daily lives creates a relay of signals across specific neurons and synapses in the brain. By experiencing something repeatedly—saying a name or phone number, seeing a face, practicing a golf swing, or making a recipe over and over again—we learn it. But how does the brain commit something to memory? When we experience something, a specific pattern of nerve cells, synapses, and neurotransmitters are activated. With each repetition, the participating cells and synapses actually begin to change and become better at relaying the signal. The neurons along the route may even sprout additional dendrites to create more and stronger synaptic connections. And in time the pattern becomes encoded in the brain as a long-term memory trace, like a well-worn path through the forest of neurons in the brain.

Research has begun to shed light on the types of physical changes that occur in the brain as a result of learning. For example, experiencing and learning lots of new things may increase:

- The development of new nerve cells in a region of the temporal lobe called the hippocampus, which is involved in learning and memory.
- The number and size of synapses—the connections between nerve cells that are necessary for relaying, processing, and recalling information.
- The amount of myelin insulation protecting the axons of nerve cells, especially in the bundle of nerves that allows the right and left sides of the brain to communicate.
- The number of tiny blood vessels that supply certain areas of the brain. More of these vessels means more blood and oxygen can flow to these areas to nourish nerve cells.
- The size and number of the glial cells that help to nourish and maintain the neurons in the brain and spinal cord.

These changes, taken together, highlight a very important feature of the brain known as plasticity. Plasticity refers to the way the brain is able to change as a result of experience. And it means that by exposing ourselves to new things and actively seeking more varied experiences on an ongoing basis, we can maintain and even enhance the brain's mental resources and cognitive abilities.

Adding On

Scientists once thought that the brain could not create new neurons once it reached adulthood. And it's true that the brain does not have the regenerative ability of, say, the skin, which is constantly creating new skin cells and shedding dead ones and has considerable ability to repair and replace damaged areas. Damaged or dead nerve cells in the brain cannot be replaced. But recent research does indicate that the brain can grow new neurons in the hippocampus, an area that plays an important role in learning and creating new memories.

The Aging Brain

Time does appear to take a toll on the brain. Once we reach our 50s and 60s, our brains slowly lose mass, especially in areas such as the frontal lobes and hippocampus. The wrinkly cerebral cortex starts to get a little thinner. The number of synapses, or connections between neurons, tends to decrease. The brain pumps out less of the neurotransmitter chemicals that ferry signals across the synapses. And the number of receptors for those chemicals appears to decrease. Still, while we lose some brain cells here and there, especially in the deeper parts of the brain, we don't typically experience significant or widespread neuron loss unless a brain disease, such as Alzheimer's, is present.

In terms of cognitive functions, increasing age tends to make us a bit slower at processing information, learning new things, and retrieving information we've already stored, although once we commit something to long-term memory, it usually stays there just as well as when we were younger. We may struggle a bit more with remembering plans we made recently. And as early as our late 20s, our ability to recall the odd fact, name, or number starts a slow roll downhill. We may also become less adept at multitasking—trying to keep track of or work on more than one thing at a time—or switching quickly from one cognitive task to another.

Still, these gradual changes in cognitive function are not inevitable. Not everyone experiences them to the same extent—or even at all. Remember, our brains and our cognitive abilities develop based on what we experience minute by minute, day by day, throughout our lives. And since no two people have exactly the same experiences (not even twins), no two brains are alike. Likewise, no two brains age—physically or functionally—in exactly the same way or at the same speed.

If you randomly invited a couple dozen healthy 70-year-olds into a room and tested their memory, problem-solving, and other cognitive abilities, you'd likely find considerable variation in the results. Most would have lost some degree of the mental sharpness they had when they were in their 20s. But some—perhaps four or five—would have barely lost a step and would perform as well or nearly as well as they did when they were in their 20s and 30s.

The point is that the brain's chronological age—the

number of years it's been on the planet—is not necessarily the same as its functional age. While genetics no doubt plays a role in such variation, scientists believe that our differing experiences and choices—not just when we're young but throughout our lives—are major factors in how well our brains age.

And that's great news, because it means that even if you're no spring chicken, you can still make choices and take steps that will revitalize, challenge, and enrich your mind so that it can start working more like it used to. The chapters that follow detail those choices and steps and provide a roadmap to follow in your quest to turn back your brain's functional age.

Protect Your Brain's Supply Lines

One of the most important ways you can help preserve and promote more youthful cognitive function throughout your life is to take good care of your brain's supply lines—the blood vessels that bring oxygen- and nutrient-rich blood to the billions of cells in your brain. That means shielding those vital supply lines by taking steps to prevent or control age-related diseases that can weaken or narrow them.

The Brain, Above All

The nerve cells in your brain, like all the other cells in your body, require an ample and steady supply of blood to deliver the oxygen and nutrients that keep them alive and fuel their activities. Compared to all those other body cells, however, the neurons in your brain are voracious consumers: Even though the brain makes up only about 2 percent of your body weight, it monopolizes roughly 20 percent of your body's blood supply. The brain's nerve cells are also among the most sensitive to a lack of oxygen. Even a brief, temporary interruption in the blood supply to your brain turns out your proverbial lights by causing you to faint. If the blood supply to the brain isn't reestablished within about four minutes, nerve cells begin to die. And once they die, they can't be replaced. The body will even sacrifice blood flow to its other organs, if necessary, to ensure sufficient blood gets to the brain. That's how important it is.

Two pairs of major blood vessels called arteries run up through your neck and into your skull to bring blood to your brain. The two on either side of the neck, near the surface, are called the carotid arteries, and the two deep within the neck are called the vertebral arteries. These arteries feed into a loop of blood vessels at the base of the brain called the circle of Willis, which in turn feeds the smaller blood vessels that branch upward from it to supply both the surface and inner depths of the brain. The circle of Willis acts, therefore, as a kind of failsafe mechanism: Even if one of the four major arteries leading into the loop fails due to blockage or rupture, blood from the other three continues to flow through the loop, feeding all of the vessels that branch off to supply blood to all of the brain's cells.

> ### Bottoms Up
>
> *Fainting may actually be nature's way of reestablishing a sufficient blood supply to the brain: It forces the heart and brain to the same horizontal plane—usually, the floor—so the heart doesn't have to fight gravity to push blood to the brain.*

BLOOD SUPPLY OF THE HEAD AND NECK

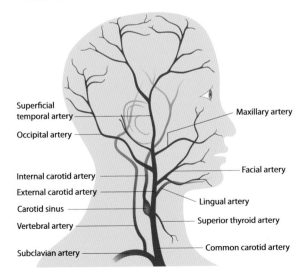

Superficial temporal artery

Occipital artery

Internal carotid artery

External carotid artery

Carotid sinus

Vertebral artery

Subclavian artery

Maxillary artery

Facial artery

Lingual artery

Superior thyroid artery

Common carotid artery

Once the cells in the brain pull the oxygen and nutrients they need from the blood, the depleted blood returns to the heart via a system of blood vessels called veins. The blood in the veins also carries cellular debris and other extraneous material away from the brain to be recycled or removed from the body. Connecting the arteries to the veins is a network of progressively tinier blood vessels called capillaries that branch off to reach every inch of the brain.

A Slowly Growing Threat

Your blood vessels are essentially tubes made of living tissue that are lined on the inside with a layer of tissue called the endothelium. The blood vessel walls start out strong and flexible, with endothelium that is smooth and unblemished, allowing blood to flow through freely and easily as the heart's contractions pump it around the body. As the years go by, however, a condition called atherosclerosis, or hardening of the arteries, can occur. Hardening of the arteries is a very common condition that often begins to develop before we even reach our teens and slowly progresses over time. Most often, it only begins to seriously threaten the brain, the heart, or other organs when we reach our 50s and 60s.

Hardening of the arteries develops when damage to the endothelium leads to a buildup of cholesterol, fats, calcium, fibrin (which plays a role in blood clotting), and other substances on the inner walls of the arteries. These deposits, which are typically covered by a hard outer layer, are called plaques. The body's immune system responds to this disease process, causing inflammation and other effects that may actually make the problem worse.

As plaque builds up, it narrows the arteries, threatening the cells and organs that depend on those blood vessels to deliver life-giving blood. When such narrowing occurs in the blood vessels that feed the brain, the brain's nerve cells can be jeopardized. The flow can become sluggish, leaving the brain's cells with less blood—and therefore less oxygen—than they need to perform well. In the worst case, the combination of plaque and inflammation can trigger a blood clot that forms or gets lodged at a narrowed area of a cerebral artery, completely cutting off blood flow or decreasing it so severely that a stroke occurs. A stroke refers to the death of neurons in areas of the brain that are cut off from their blood supply. Depending on which brain areas are damaged, the result can be paralysis, blindness, loss of speech, and/or a host of other devastating physical and cognitive disabilities. If cell death is extensive enough or occurs in especially vital areas of the brain, coma or death will occur.

Scientists are still trying to sort out the exact roles plaque and inflammation play in narrowing the arteries and causing disruption of the blood supply to the brain. But they have identified some very likely culprits behind the blood-vessel damage that gets this dangerous ball rolling.

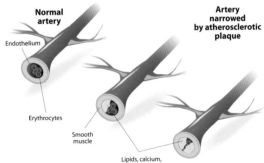

Normal artery

Endothelium

Erythrocytes

Smooth muscle

Lipids, calcium, cellular debris

Artery narrowed by atherosclerotic plaque

Stroke Fact

There are actually two major types of stroke. By far the most common, accounting for about 85 percent of all strokes, is the ischemic type. Ischemic stroke results when a blocked artery deprives brain cells of blood and the oxygen it carries. A blood clot—either one that forms in the brain artery itself or that travels there from elsewhere in the body, is the immediate cause.

The second, less common variety is the hemorrhagic stroke, which occurs when a blood vessel in the brain leaks blood or bursts, damaging brain cells in the immediate area of the leak or rupture and cutting off blood flow to the brain cells beyond that point. There are a variety of possible causes of hemorrhagic stroke, including traumatic damage to the blood vessel (from a blow to the head, for example), high blood pressure that hasn't been controlled, a malformed section of blood vessels, or an aneurysm (a balloonlike swelling in a weakened portion of an artery wall).

Supply-Line Saboteurs

Heredity and age can certainly play a role in the development of hardening of the arteries and stroke. Being African American or having a family history of cardiovascular (heart) disease or stroke, for example, puts a person at greater risk. Stroke risk also doubles every ten years after the age of 55 even when there's no genetic predisposition present. And men are more likely than women to have a stroke, although women are more likely to die from them, at least in part because they tend to be older when they experience them. These factors are out of your control, of course. But there are other contributing factors that you can do something about.

High Blood Pressure

High blood pressure, known medically as hypertension, is the number one controllable risk factor for stroke. It damages the endothelial layer of the arteries, leading to inflammation and scar-tissue formation (as the body attempts to repair the damage) and triggering the buildup of plaque that narrows the arteries that feed the brain. It can also play a role in the development of weak spots in the arteries that can lead to aneurysm.

Blood pressure refers to the force that the blood exerts on the walls of your arteries as it is pumped through them by the heart. It is expressed in two numbers, one "over" the other. The top, and higher, number refers to systolic pressure, or the pressure placed on the artery when the heart contracts (beats). The second, lower number refers to diastolic pressure, or the force placed on the artery walls between beats, when the heart is at rest.

In an adult 20 years of age or older, a systolic pressure of less than 120 mm HG and a diastolic pressure under 80 mm HG is considered normal and healthy. A systolic reading of 120 to 130 or a diastolic reading of 80 to 90 is classified as prehypertension. Stage 1 hypertension refers to a systolic reading of 140 to 159 or a diastolic reading of 90 to 99. A systolic reading of 160 or higher or a diastolic reading of 100 or higher is referred to as stage 2 hypertension. If the systolic reading climbs above 180 or the diastolic is over 110, immediate medical treatment is required, and 911 should be called at once.

The actual cause of high blood pressure, in most cases, is unknown. But scientists have discovered several factors that increase a person's risk for developing the disease. Uncontrollable risk factors include increasing age, a family history of hypertension, and being African American. But lifestyle factors including overweight, a lack of physical activity, a poor diet that includes too much salt, and alcohol abuse increase the risk of high blood pressure. Cigarette smoking, unmediated stress, and a condition called sleep apnea (marked by loud snoring and pauses in breathing during sleep) may contribute as well, although scientific research hasn't been able to confirm the connections.

Typical steps in getting blood pressure under control include:

- Adjusting the diet, especially to control calories and cut salt intake
- Getting more physical activity every day
- Cutting back on alcohol consumption
- Taking medication

High Blood Cholesterol and Triglyceride Levels

Elevated levels of cholesterol (a fatlike substance used by the body for a variety of purposes) and triglycerides (the body's storage form of excess energy) in the blood contribute to the buildup of plaque on the inner walls of arteries, including those that feed the brain. They raise the risk of stroke and heart disease, as well. While a high level of total blood cholesterol is associated with hardening of the arteries, an elevated amount of cholesterol carried through the blood in the form of low-density lipoproteins, or LDLs, is considered especially dangerous to the blood vessels. Likewise, having a low level of high-density lipoproteins—the so-called "good cholesterol" molecules responsible for removing excess cholesterol from the blood—is linked to a greater risk of blood vessel disease.

A Sneaky Assault

High blood pressure is often called a "silent killer" because it typically doesn't cause any symptoms until it has already damaged blood vessels and/or organs. More than 76 million Americans have been diagnosed with the disease, and many more have the condition without knowing it.

As is the case with blood vessel narrowing in general, cholesterol levels are affected by age, gender, and heredity. They tend to rise with increasing age. Before women reach menopause, their LDL cholesterol levels are typically lower than those of men of the same age, although after menopause, women lose their beneficial edge and may have LDL levels that are even higher than their male counterparts. There is also a form of high blood cholesterol that runs in families and can lead to hardening of the arteries, heart attack, and stroke at an earlier age.

Being inactive and, especially, being overweight tend to increase total and LDL blood cholesterol levels and lower HDL. Eating a lot of animal products, such as eggs, meat, and cheese, which naturally contain cholesterol (cholesterol is not found in plant foods) can also boost your blood cholesterol level. But ironically, far more significant than dietary cholesterol in raising total and LDL cholesterol in the blood is a diet rich in saturated and trans fats. Tran fats also lower beneficial HDL cholesterol levels.

Experts typically recommend dietary changes and increased physical activity as the first-line treatments for lowering high blood cholesterol and triglyceride levels. When such lifestyle adjustments don't bring cholesterol and triglyceride levels down low enough or fast enough, medications may be added.

How High Is Too High?

Generally, a desirable level of total blood cholesterol is under 200 mg/dL; a level from 200 to 239 mg/dL is considered borderline high, and one of 240 mg/dL or higher is classified as high. An optimal level of LDL cholesterol is less than 100 mg/dL, while a level of 100 to 129 mg/dL is considered near optimal, one of 130 to 159 mg/dL is classified as borderline high, 160 to 189 mg/dL is high, and 190 mg/dL and above is very high. In contrast, the higher the level of HDL cholesterol, the better. A level that is under 40 mg/dL is low and considered a major risk factor for hardening of the arteries, while a level of 60 mg/dL or more is thought to help lower your risk. And finally, triglyceride levels of 150 to 199 mg/dL fall into the borderline high category, and levels of 200 mg/dL or more are high and can raise your risk of having narrowed arteries.

Diabetes

Diabetes causes damage to the endothelial lining of the blood vessels. Such damage can lead to inflammation and the development of plaques that dangerously narrow the arteries that bring blood to the brain. Diabetes may encourage or speed hardening of the arteries in other ways—by aggravating inflammation within the arteries, for example—as well. The devastating result is blood vessel disease. This in turn leads to heart attack and stroke—the primary killer of people with diabetes.

Diabetes is a complex and dangerous disease that comes in two main forms, but the hallmark of both types is persistently high levels of blood glucose, or sugar. Blood sugar serves as the primary fuel for the body's cells, and insulin, a hormone produced by the pancreas, is responsible for pushing that sugar into the cells. Either a lack of insulin or a resistance to it (depending on the type of diabetes) allows the level of blood sugar to rise dangerously high and prevents the body from lowering it to normal, healthy levels.

In addition to causing damage to blood vessels, the persistently high blood sugar levels of diabetes also appear to negatively affect the brain and cognitive function in other ways, as well. For example, both Alzheimer's disease and vascular dementia are more common in people with diabetes. And research has indicated a link between prolonged high blood sugar levels and reduced performance on tests of learning, memory, other high-level cognitive abilities, and even motor function.

Diabetes is diagnosed through a series of blood tests. Roughly 15 percent of people with diabetes have the type 1, or insulin-dependent, form of the disease and must inject insulin for the rest of their lives in order to survive. They also must learn to carefully balance diet, activity, and insulin injections to prevent dangerous blood sugar highs and lows. The vast majority of people with diabetes, on the other hand, have the type 2, or non-insulin-dependent, form. Diet, physical activity level, and body weight play a role in both the development and the control of this type of diabetes. If lifestyle

TYPES OF DIABETES

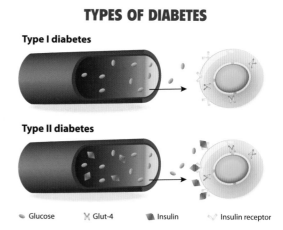

Type I diabetes

Type II diabetes

Glucose Glut-4 Insulin Insulin receptor

adjustments do not get and keep blood sugar in a healthier range, medications are prescribed; in time, insulin may be added. Working with a diabetes care team of health professionals and regularly testing blood sugar levels are essential elements of good control regardless of type.

A Common Burden

According to the latest statistics, more than 29 million Americans—that's over 9 percent of the population—suffer from diabetes. Roughly 8 million of those folks are not even aware that they have this potentially debilitating and deadly disease. In the over 65 age group, the figures are even more disheartening: More than 25 percent, or nearly 12 million seniors, have diabetes (both diagnosed and undiagnosed).

If you don't have diabetes, you and your brain are lucky. But it's wise to keep an eye out for symptoms of the condition, since the sooner high blood sugar levels are brought under control, the less chance they have to do damage throughout your body. Symptoms of diabetes include:

- *Frequent urination*
- *Unusual thirst*
- *Extreme hunger despite eating regular meals*
- *Blurry vision*

- *Extreme tiredness*
- *Slow healing of cuts and bruises*
- *Numbness, tingling, or pain in the feet and/or hands*

If you begin to notice any of these symptoms, even if they are mild at first, report them to your doctor as soon as possible.

Obesity

Obesity raises the risk of high blood pressure, type 2 diabetes, high blood triglycerides, and low HDL cholesterol, all of which can damage the blood vessels and contribute to narrowing of the arteries that supply the brain. All that excess body fat also makes it harder for the body to move blood through the blood vessels to the cells. It's not surprising, then, that hardening of the arteries occurs ten times more often in people who are obese than in those who are not. And it's not just adults who suffer brain-threatening health effects from obesity. German researchers, for example, found that 14-year-olds who were obese already had hardening of the arteries. Fortunately, the same researchers found that participating in six months of an intensive exercise regimen reversed the blood vessel damage in the youths.

Obesity has traditionally been defined as being 20 percent or more above the weight considered healthy for one's height, gender, and age. But increasingly today, overweight and obesity are defined in terms of a formula called the body mass index, or BMI. Scientists developed the BMI to help physicians determine when their patients' poundage threatened their health. The higher your BMI, the greater your risk of stroke, heart and blood vessel disease, and other killers.

Unlike the reading on your bathroom scale, the BMI takes into account your height. To determine your BMI you first need to weigh yourself and measure your height. Then, using a calculator, do the following:

1. Divide your weight in pounds by your height in inches.
2. Divide that result by your height in inches again.
3. Multiply that result by 703.

The result of this last step is your BMI.

As an example of how you would figure your BMI using this formula, let's say you weigh 190 pounds and are 5 feet 9 inches (that's 5 × 12, or 60, + 9, which equals 69 inches) tall:

1. 190 pounds ÷ 69 = 2.75
2. 2.75 ÷ 69 = 0.0399
3. 0.0399 × 703 = 28

So your BMI would be 28. But what does that mean?

According to the Centers for Disease Control and Prevention, if you are 21 years old or older, a BMI of 18.5 to 24.9 is normal, or healthy; a BMI of 25.0 to 29.9 means you are overweight; and a BMI of 30 or more means you are obese. The BMI does an accurate job of identifying people whose weight poses a health risk. (There are a few exceptions, however. For example, highly trained and muscled athletes, who tend to be at low risk of disease, often have a high BMI, because muscle is heavy and can throw off the results.) The best way to begin chipping away excess body fat is through diet changes and increased physical activity. You'll find helpful advice for doing both in chapters 3 and 4 of this book. If you are significantly overweight or obese, and especially if you already have health problems, you should work with your physician and perhaps a registered dietitian and personal trainer to plan and monitor a healthy, safe, and effective weight loss program.

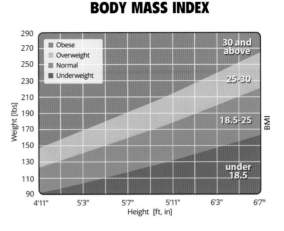

BODY MASS INDEX

Inactivity

A sedentary lifestyle puts you at risk of blood vessel disease and raises your chances of having high blood pressure, high blood cholesterol and triglycerides, low levels of protective HDL cholesterol, diabetes, and obesity. There are few other factors that threaten your brain, your blood vessels, your heart, and your entire body the way a lack of, or too little, physical activity can. Researchers have even coined a phrase for such a way of life that really gets the point across; they call it "sitting disease."

Fortunately, a lack of exercise and other physical activity is one of the easiest disease risk factors to change. To help you get moving toward a healthier brain and body, check out the advice in Chapter 4 of this book.

In addition to those we've just discussed, other controllable risk factors for hardening of the arteries include cigarette smoking, alcohol abuse, and illegal drug use, all of which are discussed in Chapter 6.

Feed Your Brain Right

The best kind of diet for feeding your brain and maintaining healthy cognitive function is . . . drumroll please! . . . the same kind of diet that's good for your heart, your blood vessels, and the rest of your body. Despite what you may have read in a magazine or heard on some late-night infomercial, there are no miracle foods or magic diet plans that will suddenly send your IQ soaring or turn your memory into a steel trap. But that doesn't mean diet isn't important to brain health and cognitive function throughout your life. And it doesn't mean that there aren't foods and nutrients that may be especially helpful in protecting your brain cells and keeping them firing on all cylinders.

So before you write off diet as a way to lower your brain's functional age, take a look at your current dietary habits and see how they compare to the advice that follows. You may be surprised to learn how much you can do at the dining table to help revitalize your brain.

Think Variety, Balance, and Moderation

These are the watchwords of a healthy diet for your brain. Your brain, like the rest of your body, requires a plethora of nutrients—such as carbohydrates, protein, fat, vitamins, and minerals—to be healthy and to function well. Because no one food or group of foods can supply all of these nutrients, the best way to ensure that you give your brain everything it needs is to eat the widest variety of foods possible.

Yes, you might consider including a multivitamin-mineral supplement as insurance, but you should still keep your food horizons wide. That's because foods contain so much more than vitamins and minerals. Plant-based foods, in particular, offer the body all sorts of phytonutrients—substances that appear to have protective effects on the body's tissues and organs. Scientists have only just begun to identify and study the many phytonutrients thought to be supplied by plant foods. And while each of these substances appears to provide benefits on its own, experts believe that they are likely most effective when consumed together in the proportions found in actual foods.

Which brings us to the second important concept in our dietary motto: balance. Your body not only needs a wide assortment of nutrients, it needs them in balance. Getting too little or too much of certain nutrients can throw others out of whack and actually hinder the way the body functions. Once again, the best way to include the proper balance your brain and body need is to consume nutrients in their natural containers— whole foods in as close to their natural state as possible.

FOOD PYRAMID

And finally, going hand in hand with balance is moderation. Too much of anything is no good, as they say, and it's true when you're eating for brain health. Even water, that life-giving fluid, can be dangerous if consumed in extremes. And while you may decide to swear off forever certain favorite foods because of their potential negative effects on your brain, you'll be more likely to stay with your healthy dietary changes if you allow yourself the occasional treat. After all, nothing makes us want something more than being told that we can never have it again. So stay away from words like "never," allow yourself the rare treat, and remember that moderation is the key to enjoyable success.

Watch Your Calorie Intake

Based on the latest government figures, 69 percent of American adults (20 years of age or older) are overweight, and just over 35 percent are obese. As mentioned in Chapter 2, people who are obese are ten times more likely to develop hardening of the arteries, which can cause a slowing or complete shutdown of blood flow to parts of the brain. Overweight and obesity increase the risk of high blood pressure, high total and LDL cholesterol levels, low HDL levels, high triglycerides, and diabetes—all major threats to the blood vessels and brain. Research also indicates that carrying excess pounds can negatively affect your brain in other ways. For example, a study published in 2012 linked overweight during middle age with poorer memory and cognitive function in later years.

So if you're a typical American dragging around extra pounds—and even more so if you fall into the obese category—you'll do your brain good now and in the future if you lose some of your excess body fat. That means getting more physically active and taking in fewer calories.

For every pound of body fat you want to lose, you need to consume 3,500 fewer calories than you burn through activity. To drop a pound a week—what experts consider a healthy rate of weight loss—you need to create a deficit of 500 calories each day. Notice, we didn't say cut 500 calories from your diet each day. It would likely be uncomfortable and difficult for you to try to shed a significant amount of body fat by cutting calories alone. That's because your body and especially your brain require a certain number of calories and a sufficient quantity and variety of foods each day to satisfy hunger and nutrient needs, fuel activities, function properly, and stay healthy. Besides, your body naturally tends to use calories more efficiently when your calorie intake falls too low; your body senses it is starving and hangs onto calories more readily to protect itself. So a combination of fewer calories and more physical activity is the safe, healthy, and effective way to go. (You'll find guidance on increasing exercise and physical activity in the next chapter.) If you can burn 150 extra calories a day by being more active, you'll only have to trim 350 calories from your daily consumption in order to achieve that pound-a-week weight loss.

> **Hey Doc!**
>
> *Before making any significant changes in your diet or activity level, it's always best to discuss your plans with your doctor and get the OK first. And if you're under the care of more than one physician—because of a chronic condition such as heart disease, high blood pressure, or diabetes, for example—be sure to check with each doctor.*

By following the advice in this chapter, especially in terms of lowering your fat and sugar intake and getting more fiber-rich foods, you will likely cut calories from your diet without even knowing it. But it's also important to start paying attention to the amount of calories in foods and, specifically, the amount of calories per serving for various foods. Check labels for calorie counts, compare products, and opt for the lower-calorie versions. You'll also want to think about how many and what kinds of nutrients you get for the calories you consume. Try to choose nutrient-dense calories rather than empty calories as often as possible.

Emphasize Whole Grains, Beans, and Fresh Fruits and Vegetables

These foods tend to be rich in nutrients, high in complex carbohydrates and fiber, and low in fat and cholesterol, so they deliver a lot of nutritional bang for your calorie buck. A diet in which these foods are center stage has been associated with a lower risk of stroke, heart and blood vessel disease, high blood cholesterol and triglycerides, high blood pressure, diabetes, and obesity.

Their carbohydrate content provides a ready source of energy for the body. As a matter of fact, carbohydrate is the only source of fuel your brain cells can use. And the fiber content of these plant foods is a boon to weight

control. Fiber passes through the body without being broken down, so it doesn't supply your body with any calories. That means you can eat larger and more filling portions of these foods without maxing out your calorie budget. Fiber also acts as nature's broom, binding with and removing excess blood cholesterol from the body and keeping food and waste moving smoothly through the digestive tract.

Their generally low fat content comes from unsaturated fats, which are better for your brain, as you'll learn in a minute. They provide a variety of amino acids, from which protein is made. Protein plays many roles in the brain (and throughout the body), including the relay of messages between neurons. And finally, these foods are packed with essential vitamins and minerals and countless phytonutrients that benefit the brain.

To help ensure that you're getting enough of these valuable foods, fill at least half, and up to two-thirds, of your plate with them. If dental or digestive issues make it uncomfortable for you to eat some fruits and

vegetables in their fresh form, it's alright to substitute stewed versions. And if you can't always get fresh produce, frozen or canned will do; just be sure to opt for plain versions (no added sugar, syrup, cream sauces, etc.), and rinse canned vegetables prior to use to remove excess sodium (commonly added as a preservative).

Your Brain Has Needs

Carbohydrates are the only source of energy your brain cells can use to fuel their work. But the brain still needs proteins and fats for other functions. Brain cells themselves, for example, consist primarily of fat molecules. And the neurotransmitters that ferry messages between nerve cells are mostly made up of amino acids, the tiny building blocks that form proteins.

Minimize Empty Calories

Candy, pastries, donuts, cakes, ice cream, and soda and other sugary beverages provide lots of calories in the form of simple sugars, and it's true the brain can use these sugars as fuel, but these foods typically provide little else of nutritional value. So including them frequently in the diet is essentially a waste of calories. What's more, many of these sweet treats also include saturated and trans fats, two types of fat that, as you'll discover shortly, can contribute to hardening of the arteries. To make sure your brain gets plenty of the nutrients that help it perform at its best, you're far better off spending your daily calorie budget on foods that actually supply those nutrients. Use fresh, ripe fruit to satisfy your sweet tooth, and keep the sugary foods and beverages filled with empty calories for the occasional treat.

Limit Fats and Choose Them Wisely

Despite its bad reputation, fat is a fundamental element of the brain and the body as a whole. It plays a variety of useful roles and is an essential part of a healthy diet.

Problems arise when we take in far more fat than we need and when we choose foods that are packed with potentially harmful types of fats.

Unlike the carbohydrates and protein we consume, which supply four calories per gram, dietary fat supplies nine calories per gram. It's a concentrated form of stored energy, which makes it extremely valuable during times of food shortage or famine. But these days, most of us in the United States suffer because we take in too many calories, not too few. A high intake of fat has been linked to overweight and obesity, which increase the risk of conditions such as high blood pressure and diabetes.

Research has also linked a high-fat diet—specifically one that is high in saturated and trans fats—to high levels of bad (LDL) cholesterol, low levels of good (HDL) cholesterol, and an increased risk of stroke and heart disease. Saturated fats and trans fats both tend to be solid at room temperature. Saturated fats occur naturally in animal products, such as red meat, poultry, and full-fat dairy products. Trans fats are primarily found in many commercially prepared cookies, pastries, pie crusts, crackers, pizza dough, baked goods, fried foods, and stick margarines (although a backlash against these fats by consumer groups has prompted some food companies to remove trans fats from their products). While trans fats occur naturally in minimal amounts in some foods, most trans fats in the American diet are created by the food industry from oils that are put through a process called partial hydrogenation; partially hydrogenating oils increases their shelf life and makes them easier to cook with.

A diet that is healthy for cells in the brain and through-out the body should instead include a moderate amount (between 20 and 30 percent or so of total calories) of monounsaturated and polyunsaturated fats, especially polyunsaturated fats that are high in a type of fatty acid called omega-3. (After all, even though these unsaturated fats tend to have a more positive effect on health, they still provide nine calories per gram and so can easily contribute to weight gain.)

Research indicates that a diet in which olive oil—which is rich in monounsaturated fats—contributes the vast majority of fat may help prevent age-related memory loss in healthy older people. Italian researchers found that senior citizens who consumed a diet high in monounsaturated fats were less likely to experience age-related decreases in thinking and memory. The more of this type of fat the subjects consumed, the greater the protection. Monounsaturated fat also appears to have a protective effect on the heart and blood vessels.

Foods that contain mostly monounsaturated fats include olives and olive oil, canola and sunflower oils, nuts, and avocado.

Similarly, polyunsaturated fats, particularly those that are high in omega-3 fatty acids, appear to benefit the health of the brain and body in a variety of ways. Research suggests that these fatty

GOOD FATS VS. BAD FATS

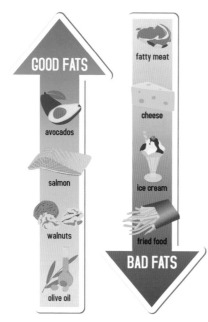

GOOD FATS

avocados

salmon

walnuts

olive oil

fatty meat

cheese

ice cream

fried food

BAD FATS

acids, found most abundantly in cold-water fish, may help lower the risk of high blood pressure, stroke, and heart disease, all of which threaten the blood supply to the brain.

Polyunsaturated fats, like their monounsaturated cousins, tend to be liquid at room temperature. Omega-3 fatty acids are found in certain plant foods, including walnuts, sunflower seeds and sunflower oil, soybean and soybean oil, canola oil, and ground flaxseed, although the body can't use them as well as the omega-3s that come from fish. Cold-water fish rich in these fatty acids include herring, mackerel, salmon, sardines, trout, and tuna.

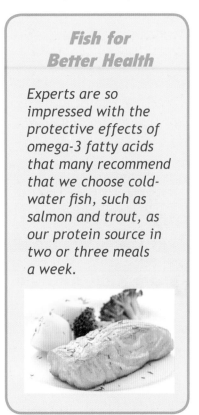

Fish for Better Health

Experts are so impressed with the protective effects of omega-3 fatty acids that many recommend that we choose cold-water fish, such as salmon and trout, as our protein source in two or three meals a week.

The following tips can help you begin to lower your total fat intake and replace unhealthy saturated and trans fats with beneficial unsaturated fats:

- Trim the visible marbling from meats, and choose leaner cuts, such as round and loin cuts, over well-marbled cuts such as rib and shoulder cuts. Keep in mind that when it comes to the grade of beef, veal, and lamb, "prime" cuts have the most fat, "choice" have less, and "good" the least.
- Limit fatty and salty luncheon meats and other high-fat processed meats, including hot dogs, bacon,

and sausage; more than half their calories come from fat, and most of that is saturated.

- Trim the skin and visible fat from poultry, and limit goose and duck, which are very high in saturated fat.
- Choose fish (especially cold-water types); white-meat poultry without the skin; and beans, nuts, and other legumes more often than red meat and pork as your protein source in a meal. And try using meat as a topping or accent to pasta and rice dishes instead of making it the main entrée.
- Instead of frying meat and poultry, try baking, broiling, or roasting. When basting, use wine, lemon juice, or tomato juice instead of the fatty drippings from the meat or poultry itself.
- Purchase tuna or other fish packed in water rather than oil. If water-packed isn't available, rinse the fish before eating.
- Opt for fat-free and low-fat versions of dairy products, and try substituting plain nonfat yogurt for sour cream as a topping.
- Choose low-fat versions of foods when available, but before you put a product in your cart, compare the calories per serving of the low-fat and regular versions to be sure the low-fat version is actually lower in calories as well. (Some food manufacturers make up for the loss of flavor from fat by adding more sugar or salt.)
- Avoid spoiling whole grains, vegetables, fish, and lean meats with cream, butter, or cheese sauce.

Common Sources of Saturated Fat and Cholesterol

Animal fats (bacon fat, chicken fat, etc.)
Butter
Cocoa butter
Coconut and coconut oil
Cream
Egg yolks
Hardened fat or oil
Hydrogenated vegetable oil
Lard
Palm and palm kernel oil
Vegetable shortening
Whole milk solids

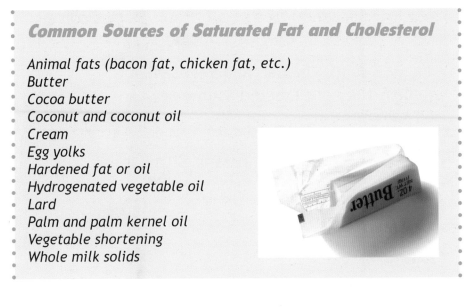

Cut Back on Sodium

As we mentioned in Chapter 2, sodium can cause an increase in blood pressure in some people, and high blood pressure can damage the arteries leading to the brain. Since there is currently no laboratory test that can determine whose blood pressure will rise too high in response to excess sodium in the diet, most experts recommend that we all cut back. The body only needs about 400 milligrams of sodium a day, yet the typical American consumes more than 3,000 milligrams daily, so why take the risk?

Surprisingly, the salt shaker contributes only a small part of our sodium overage. Many processed and prepared foods—which have become staples in our too-busy-to-cook society—are packed with the stuff. According to one estimate, Americans get more than 75 percent of their sodium from prepared or processed foods. And it's not only from foods that taste salty, like deli meats and hot dogs. A fast-food cherry pie may actually contain twice as much sodium as a small order of fries! Other sources of sodium to watch for include:

- Canned soups, beans, and vegetables (unless they are labeled as low or no sodium)
- Frozen foods
- Breakfast cereals and instant oatmeal
- Condiments
- Pickles
- Seasonings
- Antacids

Fortunately, we can unlearn our taste for salt by gradually cutting back on high-sodium foods for a few weeks. Here are some strategies that will help:

- Choose foods that say "reduced sodium" or "no salt" on the package.
- If you can't find no-salt canned vegetables or beans, rinse them before cooking to remove some of the sodium.
- Substitute fresh produce for processed or fast foods as often as possible.
- Make soup at home from scratch so you can avoid all the sodium found in so many of the canned and prepared varieties. Consider making a large pot of it and freezing smaller portions for use when time is tighter.
- Get creative with herbs and spices to add some zing to bland foods.
- Taste your food before adding salt or salty condiments; additional salt may not be necessary.
- Tell restaurant servers you want your food prepared without MSG or high-sodium ingredients.

Select a Rainbow of Produce

As we mentioned at the start of this chapter, eating a wide variety of foods is a way to ensure that your brain and body get plenty of the essential nutrients and protective phytonutrients that can help keep them functioning well as the years go by. That advice is just as important when it comes to fruits and vegetables.

Many kinds of produce provide vitamin C, beta-carotene (a form of vitamin A), flavonoids, and/or other phytonutrients that have anti-inflammatory and antioxidant powers. Inflammation, as we discussed in Chapter 2, is thought to be a major contributor to hardening of the arteries, which can compromise the blood flow to the brain. Inflammation likely also plays some role in the development of Alzheimer's disease. Anti-inflammatory compounds in fruits and vegetables fight against such inflammation.

Antioxidant compounds in foods help to defend the body's cells, including those in the brain and blood-vessel lining, from damage caused by oxidation (the same process that causes metal to rust). Oxidation occurs naturally in the body, as cells use oxygen for

> ### Get the Blues ...and Reds
>
> *Research indicates that eating lots of blueberries and strawberries appears to slow cognitive decline in older folks, delaying it by as much as 2.5 years. Both fruits are loaded with phytonutrients called flavonoids that have anti-inflammatory and antioxidant powers. Getting more total flavonoids was also associated with an actual reduction in the degeneration of cognitive function that typically occurs as we get older.*

various functions, but it also results from exposure to toxins and other insults, such as cigarette smoke and certain illegal drugs and air pollutants. The body uses antioxidants to protect its cells from such damage, but sometimes the oxidative stress overwhelms the body's defensive resources, causing cell damage that can eventually lead to stroke, heart disease, cancer, or other medical problems. Consuming a diet rich in antioxidants helps to strengthen the body's defenses and so may prevent or lessen physical deterioration in the brain due to aging.

In general, the deeper or darker the color of the produce, the greater its phytonutrient content. Fruits that fall into this category include berries, cherries, red grapes, raisins, plums and prunes, and oranges and nectarines. Examples of dark- or deep-colored vegetables include broccoli, brussels sprouts, spinach, kale, beets, corn, onions, and peppers.

Armed with the nutrition advice we've provided in this chapter, you can make dietary choices that will do a better job of

Go Nuts!

A small handful of unsalted nuts, including almonds, hazelnuts, pecans, pine nuts, peanuts (which are actually legumes, not true nuts), and/or walnuts makes a great brain-smart snack. They're a good source of filling protein and a great source of vitamin E, an antioxidant that can help shield your brain cells from damage. Plus, most of their fat is the beneficial monounsaturated variety. But that fat still packs quite a calorie load, so don't overfill your hand or reach for seconds.

providing your brain with the nutrients it needs to function well today and in the future and ward off the damage that can occur as you age. There's no time like the present to begin adopting this advice, either, because as you learn more about how to challenge your brain and keep it in tip-top shape, it's going to get hungry. Feed it right!

Stay Liquid

Your body is 60 percent water, the blood that carries oxygen and nutrients to your brain is roughly 80 percent water, and your brain itself is 70 percent water. If you lose just 2 to 4 percent of your body's water, you'll have trouble thinking straight. Water also helps your body regulate its temperature and al-lows your joints to move comfortably. Indeed, it's hard to overstate how essential water is to the human body. Yet as we get older, the body's low-water signal—the thirst mechanism—can become less sensitive, leaving us vulnerable to dehydration. So it's crucial to take in plenty of water throughout the day, even if you're not feeling particularly parched.

Since 80 percent of our water intake typically comes from beverages—the other 20 percent comes from foods—it's important to drink plenty of fluids. Water is the best bet, but other beverages add to the total as well. Even caffeinated beverages, such as coffee, tea, and some sodas pitch in; although caffeine has a dehydrating effect—it promotes water loss from the body through urine—the effect is relatively short-lived and unlikely to cause a net loss of water. Still, plain water should be your go-to beverage. The Institute of Medicine recommends nine glasses for the average adult woman and 13 for the average man each day. Of course, in hot and dry conditions, the body loses water more quickly as it works to keep its temperature in a safe range, so water needs may be somewhat higher.

Move It or Lose It

Spending the day doing chores like mopping the floor, cycling to the post office, washing the windows, raking the leaves, and walking the dog may leave you rubbing your tired muscles and grumbling about feeling old, but it may be one of the most effective steps you can take to keep your brain from showing its age.

That's right. As surprising as it may seem, if you want to preserve good brain health and cognitive function as you grow older, you need to move your muscles. More precisely, you need to become more physically active every day and regularly engage in aerobic exercise—the kind that gets your heart and lungs working harder to meet your moving muscles' increased demands for oxygen.

Exercise can help improve just about every aspect of your physical health, from boosting your cardiovascular fitness to lowering your risk of certain cancers. Experts have known for years that being more physically active lowers the risk of multiple medical issues that jeopardize the health of your brain, including obesity, diabetes, high blood pressure, low HDL cholesterol, hardening of the arteries, heart attack, and stroke. Regular exercise is also an essential part of controlling, treating, and/or recovering from these conditions. And now, based on a body of evidence that continues to expand, we know that being physically active can help lower the risk of Alzheimer's disease and other dementias and keep your mind sharp even into old age.

Some of the earliest research in this area, conducted in the 1990s on mice, showed that animals given time to run on a treadmill grew twice as many new neurons in the hippocampal region of their brains as did mice that didn't have access to treadmills. The hippocampus is a key player in learning and memory. When the researchers went back and taught both groups of mice how to navigate a maze, they found that the mice that exercised were quicker to learn and ended up taking a shorter path to the maze's end compared to the less active mice.

In another study, one group of middle-aged and older monkeys ran on a treadmill for an hour a day five days a week and another group simply sat on the machine for the same amount of time. In subsequent testing, the monkeys that exercised were twice as quick to learn new things as were the monkeys who were couch—or is that treadmill?—potatoes. The exercise benefit held true for even the oldest of the monkeys. The research further indicated that the active older monkeys only held on to their cognitive edge if they continued to exercise; with just a three-month break from exercise, the beneficial brain changes from activity disappeared.

Research with people points to a very similar relationship between physical activity and cognition. Studies have found, for example, that people who exercise frequently have a distinctive brain-wave pattern characterized by steep peaks and valleys, which is associated with alertness. These active folks are better at focusing and blocking out distractions, which in turn means that they are better able to pay attention to information that they want to remember and better at retrieving those memories as needed. Research has also found that aerobic exercise can help maintain short-term memory, especially verbal memory, which is important when you want to recall names, directions, and phone numbers, or match a name with a face. It also appears to greatly benefit functions such as planning, scheduling, and multitasking.

Make Your Days More Active

A simple way to start turning an inactive life into a more active one is to start small. Try some of these suggestions for including more physical movement into your days:

- Walk around your house, yard, or office while talking on the phone.
- When meeting up with friends, walk and chat instead of just sitting.
- Use stairs instead of elevators and escalators, especially when you're only going up or down a level or two. If you're going farther than that, get off a couple floors early and take the stairs the rest of the way.
- For nearby errands, leave the car in the garage and walk or take a bicycle.
- If you drive to work or to go shopping, choose the farthest parking spot from the building's entrance.

- At work, take a five-minute walk outside or even around the building itself instead of just sitting down during break times. Split your lunch hour and spend half eating your lunch and the other half taking a walk or climbing stairs.
- Instead of calling or emailing a coworker who sits in a different area of the building, walk over to them to ask a question or deliver information.
- Walk down every aisle of the grocery store, even if you only need a couple of things. (If you're worried about being tempted into buying sweets or snacks you don't need, just skip those specific aisles.)
- Take your dog for a walk two or even three times a day. If you don't own a dog, consider adopting one, volunteering as a dog walker at a shelter, or asking a neighbor if you can tag along as they walk theirs.
- Walk on a treadmill or just walk in place as you watch TV.
- Do your own housework (skip the robotic vacuum) and yard work. Consider using a push mower instead of one powered by electricity or gas.
- Wash your car the old-fashioned way—with a hose, a bucket, soap, and a sponge. Give yourself a real workout by waxing it by hand, too.
- Instead of going out to movies or shows, do something active like dancing, bowling, or playing miniature golf. Spend an hour or two strolling a museum, craft show, or flea market.
- Walk the grandkids around the zoo or a park, fly a kite with them, or join in their game of hide-and-seek.
- Take up an active hobby, such as bird-watching, metal detecting, woodworking, or gardening. Try recruiting friends for weekly games of bocce,

horseshoes, or table tennis.
- Practice yoga, pilates, tai chi, or some other form of relaxing movement. Virtually every health club, YMCA, and adult education program offers classes that teach such activities. Many hospitals do, as well.

Get in the Exercise Habit

Adding more movement to your days in such simple ways can certainly get you out of your easy chair and help you burn some extra calories. But it's not enough if you really want to revitalize and protect your brain. For that, you'll need to regularly engage in physical activities that are a bit more challenging. In other words, you'll need to exercise. And you'll need that exercise to be aerobic, meaning it works the large muscles of your arms, legs, and buttocks in repetitive movement and raises your heart and breathing rates for an extended period of time.

Aerobic exercise is the type that has shown so many positive health effects for your brain and blood vessels as well as your body as a whole. That's not to say that other forms of exercise, such as strength training or yoga, aren't beneficial. But to generate the kind of anti-aging changes we've talked about in this chapter, you need to perform aerobic exercise several days a week. Researchers confirmed this when they studied two groups of sedentary (but otherwise healthy) adults aged 55 to 80. One group walked for 40 minutes three days a week for a year while the other engaged in strengthening and balance exercises for the same amount of time. The hippocampus region of the brain normally loses about 2 percent of its size each year as we age. When the researchers used MRI to scan the brains of the two groups at the end of the study, they discovered that the hippocampus in folks who walked actually increased an average of 2 percent in size, while those who did the strengthening and balance activities lost 1 percent of their hippocampal volume. It's important to note two other findings that came out of this study. One is that an aerobic activity as simple and accessible as walking can help keep the brain young. The other is that even adults who only begin exercising regularly in their later years can reap its benefits for the brain.

Go Long!

When you're exercising to lose weight as well as to protect and enhance your cognitive function, what's most important is the total number of calories you burn each day. That's why almost any kind of physical activity above and beyond what you normally do can move you closer to your goal.

Of course, 30 minutes of jogging will burn more calories than 30 minutes of walking. But that's mainly because the number of calories you burn is roughly equivalent to your weight times the distance you cover, and you simply cannot cover as much ground in 30 minutes by walking as you can by jogging. To bring the calorie-burning benefit of a walk closer to that of a jog, therefore, you need to cover more ground, and to do that, you need to walk for a longer period of time. So if you're a beginning fitness walker who wants to lose weight, you should focus on building up to an hour or more of walking time every day or most days of the week. If that sounds too intimidating, keep in mind that you can split that one-hour walk into two or even three shorter brisk walks throughout the day.

What to Do

The specific type(s) of aerobic exercise you choose to incorporate into your life should be based on what you like to do, what you have easy access to, and what will be safe and reasonable given your current health, abilities, and schedule. Generally speaking, low-impact aerobic exercises are best, especially if you haven't exercised regularly in a long time. These are activities that don't involve a lot of jumping, pounding, or hitting anything with lots of force (which can damage muscles, bones, and joints). Examples include brisk walking, swimming, cycling, hiking, rowing, stair climbing, using an elliptical or similar training machine, low-impact water aerobics, and dancing.

If your fitness level allows, however, you can include various court sports (tennis, racquetball, squash, or basketball, for example) as well as higher-impact activities, such as running, jumping rope, or martial arts.

Even those who have mobility or balance issues or problems with their lower extremities (such as poor circulation or nerve damage from diabetes) can get a beneficial workout through non-weight-bearing aerobic exercise. Good choices may include riding an exercise bike, exercising in water, armchair aerobics (you can often find CDs or programs at your local hospital or even on morning cable television that show you how to do these), or pedaling an arm ergometer (which is like a bicycle for your arms).

For most folks, brisk walking is a staple of their aerobic exercise routine because it's flexible, accessible, and safe, and everyone knows how to do it. When the weather permits, it can be done outside through neighborhoods (yours or others in your city or town) or at a local park or high school track. During inclement weather, your walking workout can be taken indoors on a treadmill or at a local mall, health club, or YMCA. A walking routine can typically be kept up even when you're away from home on a business trip or vacation. And you can keep it fresh and interesting by varying the location of your walks or by walking with a family member or friend or even with a group of fellow walkers.

Even if walking is your go-to exercise of choice, however, you may want to intersperse other aerobic activities, preferably ones that challenge different or additional muscles. This is called cross-training. It can help you develop well-rounded fitness and minimize soreness from overuse of the same muscles and joints.

Calories Burned per Mile of Walking

If you walk one mile at a moderate pace (in the range of 2 to 3.5 miles per hour) and:

You Weigh	You'll Burn Roughly
120 lbs	65-70 calories
140 lbs	75-80 calories
160 lbs	85-90 calories
180 lbs	95-100 calories
200 lbs	105-115 calories
220 lbs	115-125 calories
250 lbs	130-140 calories
275 lbs	145-155 calories
300 lbs	155-170 calories

When and How Often

When choosing a time of day to exercise, focus on convenience. For long-term success, pick a time of day that works with your schedule and lifestyle. If your schedule varies too much for you to be able to establish one set time to exercise each day, so be it. The main point is that you want to treat your exercise time as an essential part of your day or week, not something you do only when you feel like. It's far too important, and you need to make the time for it.

Put It in Writing

To help ensure that you fit exercise into your busy life, make a daily appointment for it in your calendar. Actually write it down or type it in ahead of time just as you would for a business meeting or doctor appointment. It really is that important to your well-being now and for years to come.

Beyond convenience, you probably want to ensure that you do not exercise strenuously too close to bedtime. Getting your heart and blood pumping and your breathing rate and body temperature up through exercise within two or three hours of bedtime may make

it more difficult for your to fall asleep. Better to schedule your exercise earlier. Then again, it's perfectly fine to do your aerobic workout during the day and also take a pleasant, leisurely stroll after dinner or just before turning in. Many people find this to be a relaxing part of their nighttime ritual, one that also helps their digestion.

How Often

To maximize the potential health benefits of aerobic exercise, you should do it just about every day of the year. And once you make exercise part of your routine, you may actually find that you miss it on days when you can't do it, due to illness or injury, for instance. But if you've been inactive for quite a while or never exercised regularly before, an everyday commitment to working out may feel far too daunting, at least at this point.

Not to worry. First of all, you should never go from getting no physical activity to putting in a lengthy daily workout overnight. It's something you need to build up to gradually. When you're just getting started, aim for three days a week, which is pretty much the minimum you'll need to put in to get significant cognitive and health benefits. Then gradually, over the span of several weeks, increase the number of days until you're exercising five, six, or all seven days a week.

> **Wait!**
>
> *Before you begin any form of exercise, be sure to run your plans by your physician(s), especially if you haven't been active recently or have any serious health issues.*

How Intensely

Forget "no pain, no gain." Pain means you're overdoing it or doing something improperly. Exercise should feel good. If it doesn't, ease up.

Moderate intensity is what you want to aim for. That

means not too easy and not too hard—just right smack in the middle. There are a couple of methods you can use to judge whether you're in the middle: measuring your heart rate and using the "talk test."

You can take your pulse either at your wrist or, if you don't press too hard, on the side of your Adam's apple. (Check your pulse a few times throughout the activity, without stopping if possible; otherwise, stop the activity only long enough to count the heartbeats.) Counting your pulse for ten seconds will let you know if you are above, below, or within what is called your target heart-rate range during exercise. If your pulse count during exercise is above the range listed in the table shown here, slow down. If it is below, speed up a bit. Keep in mind that even if you maintain the exact same intensity, your pulse rate may go up during the course of a workout as you begin to fatigue, so check your pulse every five or ten minutes throughout your workout to ensure you're still in your target range.

Your Age	Ten-Second Target Heart-Rate Range
20-29	20-26
30-39	19-25
40-49	18-23
50-59	17-22
60-69	16-21
70-79	15-19
80 or above	14-18

The other way to track the intensity of your effort during exercise is called the "talk test," a practical, if rather unscientific method that should still help you pace yourself properly. It relies on this simple guideline: You should be able to hold a conversation, but not be able to sing, when exercising at the right intensity. If you have difficulty doing this, you're working too hard. If you can belt out a few verses of your favorite song, you need to pick up your pace. What could be simpler?

For How Long

If you have not exercised in many years (or ever), it is fine to start out at an easy pace for just a few minutes at a time and then gradually build up the length of your exercise session by adding one minute each time you exercise. You should aim to reach a minimum of 30 minutes of continuous exercise, although it would be best if you could gradually work up to one 60-minute exercise session or two 30-minute sessions each day.

Once you have reached the desired workout length, start to slowly increase your speed or intensity. This will allow you to get and keep your heart rate in your target range as your fitness improves, and it will keep your workouts challenging and stimulating.

Start and End Slowly

Your 30 to 60 minutes of exercise per day should include a few minutes of warm-up and cool-down time spent in a slow, easy version of your chosen exercise. If you plan to walk briskly for exercise, for example, start and finish your workout with three to five minutes of casual walking. This allows your heart rate to adjust gradually and safely as you begin and end your workout. It may also help to minimize soreness and prevent injury by allowing your muscles to warm up and cool down, as well.

Give It a Rest

Your brain never really stops working, even when you are asleep. As a matter of fact, when you're sleeping, it continues its job of keeping your basic body systems running smoothly.

This sleepy time cleanup routine is essential to alertness, concentration, learning, and memory during your waking hours. If you don't get enough quality sleep, your brain and cognitive functions suffer. Recent research in mice has found that lack of sleep can actually cause permanent damage to and even kill nerve cells in the brain, specifically a type that helps to keep us awake and aware. (The researchers believe similar damage occurs in the brains of humans who stay awake too long, too.)

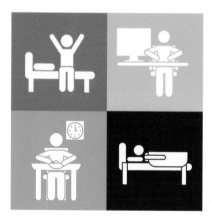

So ensuring that you get enough high-quality sleep is not only important for your body, it's key to the health of your brain and your ability to think, learn, and remember.

You've Got Rhythms

Before the invention of electricity, people went to bed shortly after the sun went down. Sure, it sounds boring, but there was a predictable rhythm to life that was dictated by sunshine and darkness. But in modern times, we tend to move to a different beat. Our frenetic lifestyles have disrupted the traditional rhythms of sleep. Sleep now competes against work and other commitments, along with a host of entertainment options. This creates challenges for us in terms of getting the rest we need.

Fortunately, we have a built-in body clock that attempts to keep us in step with a normal 24-hour cycle of waking and sleeping. This body clock is often referred to as the circadian rhythm. It is our body's natural way of trying to regulate not only our sleep patterns but a variety of other bodily processes, including digestion, elimination, growth, renewal of cells, and body temperature. When we work with our body's natural cycle, we can greatly improve not only our sleep but our overall health. When we fight against that cycle, on the other hand, our sleep, waking performance, and health can suffer.

What Happens During Sleep?

It was widely believed until about midway through the twentieth century that there was only one type of sleep. Whether you got one hour or ten hours of sleep, it was the same garden variety. And that is how most people still think of sleep today. But since the invention of modern machines that can monitor our sleep patterns, we have learned that there are actually two main kinds of sleep—an important discovery that has helped us gain insight into what happens during sleep.

One kind of sleep is called rapid-eye-movement (REM)

sleep. It gets its name from the distinctive shifting of the eyes that occurs when you are in this state. The second kind is termed non-REM (NREM) sleep, during which the distinctive rapid eye movements are absent. NREM sleep is often very deep, involving both mental and physical inactivity. As you sleep, you cycle in and out of REM and NREM.

NREM sleep is further divided into four stages. You repeatedly pass through these stages for different lengths of time during a typical night's sleep. When you finally awaken, you have covered much ground without being aware of it. Had you been physically active all that time, you would be exhausted. But, interestingly, this very cycling through stages is what renews your body and mind while you sleep.

Sleep Monitoring

You might wonder how researchers can accurately tell you what is happening in your mind and body while you doze. After all, since you're asleep, they can't ask you. So scientists came up with an alternative. They developed a test called polysomnography, which monitors electrical activity in the brain, eye movement, muscle activity, heart rate, air flow, chest and stomach movements, and blood-oxygen levels that occur while you sleep. Electrodes (small adhesive patches with wires attached) are placed on your scalp and other parts of your body to record this activity. The results can give sleep specialists a very accurate picture of what is happening in your body, because different stages of sleep are marked by distinct brain waves and physical responses. This test is used to help diagnose certain sleep disorders.

Sleep States

NREM Stage One

This first stage of NREM sleep is where you transition from wakefulness to sleep. It lasts only five to ten minutes for most people. Your brain waves, breathing, heart rate, body temperature, and metabolic rate slow down, and your muscles relax. You can be awakened easily out of this stage of sleep, and if this happens, you may feel as if you haven't slept at all yet. Most people only spend about five percent of their total sleeping time in this stage.

NREM Stage Two

In stage two, you enter a light-medium level of sleep. You usually spend about 45 to 50 percent of your total sleep time in stage two. During this stage, you can still be awakened easily.

NREM Stage Three

Your brain progressively slows down as you drift into deeper sleep. Your muscles become limp, and breathing is slow and steady. Stage three and stage four sleep are sometimes referred to together as deep sleep because body functions are similar during each. You spend a total of about 20 to 25 percent of your total sleep time in stages three and four. Attempting to awaken someone from this stage can be more difficult; they may experience a few moments of grogginess before they fully awaken.

NREM Stage Four

This is the deepest stage of sleep. It is during this time that your heart rate, breathing, metabolism, and temperature are at their lowest. Waking someone from this stage of sleep can take a good deal of effort. During the four stages of NREM sleep, you progressively drift into a state of deeper sleep. It takes most people from 90 to 120 minutes to pass through all four stages.

The REM Sleep State

It is in the REM sleep state that you do most of your dreaming. When you dream, your eyes involuntarily move back and forth in a rapid fashion. Some researchers believe that our eyes are moving this way in an effort to "watch," or follow, action that is occurring in our dreams. The REM state "looks" lighter than the deeper stages of NREM sleep because the brain waves during REM resemble those in NREM stage one and in wakefulness. But REM sleep is actually considered to be a deep and restorative state, necessary for higher brain function and memory. REM sleep was once called paradoxical sleep because it looked like sleep subjects in this state were awake or only lightly sleeping. In reality, subjects in REM sleep proved hard to awaken. It was only after the discovery of rapid eye movements in 1953 that this distinct state of sleep was defined and renamed.

Here's how the various sleep states fit together: As you go from stage one to stage four of NREM sleep, your brain and body become increasingly more relaxed. Once you reach REM sleep, however, both brain and body functions switch gears. Your heart rate and breathing speed up, and your fingers, face, and legs may twitch. These responses are indicators that your brain is in a more active state. Fortunately, while all of this activity is going on in your brain, your body is almost paralyzed.

You cycle in and out of REM sleep throughout the night. The length of each REM period gradually increases during the night, with the first period lasting about ten minutes and the final period lasting 40 to 60 minutes. After the first REM period, you return to stage two and work your way back to REM for a slightly longer amount of time. Over the course of the night, you will cycle through these stages four to six times, depending on how long you sleep. If you awaken during the night, it is usually when you are completing a cycle out of REM and are on your way back to stage two. When you do awaken, you most likely fall back to sleep immediately without realizing the break in your sleep.

It is this cycling through the various states of sleep, and especially the time spent in REM sleep, that determines how rested you feel when you wake up. This also explains why people who do not get the amount of  sleep they need feel so tired. They have not spent an adequate amount of time cycling through the stages of NREM sleep and have cut the time they have spent in REM sleep. The body can compensate for short periods of sleep deprivation, but long or chronic patterns of sleep loss have detrimental effects.

Age and Sleep

Answer true or false about the following statement: Seniors don't need as much sleep as they did when they were younger. Most people would say "true." And most people would be wrong. It is a myth that seniors need less sleep simply because they are older. Older adults require the same six to nine hours of restful sleep as other adults. The stumbling blocks for seniors in getting this amount of sleep include poor lifestyle habits and chronic illness, both of which can disrupt sleep.

It used to be thought that the internal body clock of older people required them to get less sleep. Research has shown this notion to be false. It is true that seniors tend to rise earlier in the morning and become sleepy in the afternoon. This is due to the internal body clock setting itself to a different rhythm as we age. Social factors, such as going to bed early out of boredom, and medical illnesses and medications that cause fatigue and sleepiness, may also cause earlier bedtimes and therefore early morning awakening.

Set the Stage for Better Sleep

In order to maximize your sleep time, there are four main considerations. You must:

- Begin your preparations for sleep during the day
- Schedule your sleep patterns deliberately
- Practice habits that help your body to relax before sleep
- Control your sleep environment

Prepare for Sleep All Day

From the moment you wake up in the morning, you have choices to make that can affect how well you sleep that night. Making wise choices throughout the day can help you sleep soundly at night and awaken with renewed energy.

1. Exercise to Sleep Better

The majority of people claim that they don't exercise on a regular basis because they are too tired. Hmmm. Could that have something to do with sleep habits, perhaps? Chances are good that it does. If there were a competition to determine which lifestyle habit would win the title of "best intention never acted on," exercise would probably win. The reason we intend to exercise is that we all know how good it is for us. And research finds new benefits every day. Regular exercise improves heart health and blood pressure, builds bone and muscle, helps combat stress and muscle tension, and can even improve mood. Add one more benefit: sound sleep. Did you know that exercise can help you sleep sounder and longer? It's true. But the key is found in the type of exercise you choose and the time you participate in it during the day. What time of the day do you think exercise would best help you sleep? Morning? Afternoon? Evening? Right before bed?

Exercising vigorously right before bed or within about three hours of your bedtime can actually make it harder to fall asleep. This surprises many people; it's often thought that a good workout before bed helps you feel more tired. In actuality, vigorous exercise right before bed stimulates your heart, brain, and muscles—the opposite of what you want at bedtime. It also raises your body temperature right before bed, which, you'll soon discover, is not what you want.

Morning exercise can relieve stress and improve mood. These effects can indirectly improve sleep, no doubt. To get a more direct sleep-promoting benefit from morning exercise, however, you can couple it with exposure to outdoor light.

When it comes to having a direct effect on getting a good night's sleep, it's vigorous exercise in the late afternoon or early evening that appears most beneficial. That's because it raises your body temperature above normal a few hours before bed, allowing it to start falling just as you're getting ready for bed. This decrease in body temperature appears to be a trigger that helps ease you into sleep.

The type of vigorous workout we're talking about is a cardiovascular workout. That means you engage in some activity in which you keep your heart rate up and your muscles pumping continuously for at least 20 minutes. Although strength-training, stretching, yoga, and other methods of exercise are beneficial, none match the sleep-enhancing benefits of cardiovascular exercise.

The Exercise-Sleep Connection

Everyone's body temperature naturally goes up slightly in the daytime and back down at night, reaching its low just before dawn. Decreasing body temperature seems to be a trigger, signaling the body that it's time to sleep. Vigorous exercise temporarily raises the body temperature as much as two degrees. Twenty or 30 minutes of aerobic exercise is sufficient to keep the body temperature at this higher level for a period of four to five hours, after which it drops lower than if you hadn't exercised. This lower body temperature is what helps you sleep better. So if you exercise five to six hours before going to bed, you will be attempting to sleep at the same time your temperature is beginning to go down. That's the best way to maximize exercise's beneficial effects on sleep.

2. Brighten Your Morning

Light tells the brain it is time to wake up. That's probably obvious to anyone who has had to turn on a light in the middle of the night and then has had trouble getting back to sleep. What may not be so obvious is that exposure to light at other times, particularly in the early morning, can actually help you sleep at night.

How does morning light improve sleep? The light helps to regulate your biological clock and keep it on track. This internal clock is located in the brain. There does, however, appear to be a kind of forward drift built into the brain. By staying up later and, more importantly, getting up later, you reinforce that drift, which means you may find you have trouble getting to sleep and waking up when you need to. To counter this forward drift, you need to reset your clock each day, so that it

stays compatible with the earth's 24-hour daily rhythm—
and with your daily schedule. Exposing yourself to light
in the morning appears to accomplish this resetting.
Many factors can affect our biological clock, but light
appears to be the most important. The timing of
exposure is crucial; the body clock is most responsive
to sunlight in the early morning, between 6:00 and 8:30
A.M. Exposure to sunlight later does not provide the
same benefit. The type of light also matters, as does the
length of exposure. Direct sunlight outdoors for at least
one-half hour produces the most benefit. The indoor
lighting in a typical home or office has little effect.

3. Manage Stress

If you moved into a new neighborhood only to discover
that it was plagued by smelly smoke from a nearby
factory, you would likely be annoyed or angry at first.
But after several weeks, you probably wouldn't notice
it as much. You would become conditioned to the smell
despite the fact that it may not be terribly healthy for
you. A similar phenomenon can occur when we
experience stress on an ongoing basis. We may be so
bombarded with daily stress that we become
accustomed to it. But such constant exposure to stress
can make it difficult to get needed sleep and can
compromise our overall health.

It's important to dispel the myth that you can avoid
stress. If you breathe, you are going to encounter life
situations that bring stress. Since you can't avoid it, the
best option is to learn to manage it. One key to
managing stress is assessing what you have control over
and what you don't. For instance, if your boss has set an
unrealistic deadline for a project, you may have little or

no control over changing that. But you do have control over how you respond to that deadline. And your response to a given situation is what you want to focus on as you seek to manage stress. You can choose to do certain things and not others. This ability to choose puts you in control and gives you the ability to make the situation work for you.

Professional therapists who specialize in stress reduction will tell you that your body is the best guide to determining when you are feeling stressed. If you pay attention to how you feel both physically and emotionally, you can often intervene before stress begins to interfere with sleep.

What does stress management during the day have to do with sleeping well at night? Plenty. Have you ever had the unpleasant experience of crawling into bed exhausted and spending the next few hours tossing and turning as you go over every detail of your day? That is stress at work on your mind. All of those emotions and thoughts throughout the day that were not dealt with at the time can work their way to the surface in the quiet of night.

In addition, the more you dwell on the upsetting events, the greater the effect on your body. When it senses stress, the brain sends a message to the body to release hormones that heighten alertness and prepare it for action. This is known as the fight-or-flight response. It's a beneficial reaction if you need to fight off a dog that threatens you on your walk or jump out of the way of a speeding vehicle. But when the stress is mental and there is no physical response necessary, that heightened state of alertness can keep you from relaxing enough to sleep. By learning to deal with stressors in your life more immediately during the day, you are less likely to be kept awake by them at night. Later in this chapter, we'll talk about ways to further release yourself from the stress response as you prepare for bed.

4. Don't Procrastinate

Many of us are great procrastinators, living by the motto "Why do today what I can put off until tomorrow?" If you're a procrastinator, you can't afford to put off reading this section. Putting work, projects, or tasks off almost always has bad consequences, one of which is disturbed sleep. Getting your work done can be seen as another way of managing your stress. You can choose to put your time and energy into accomplishing what is before you and reap the benefits or put it off and worry about it. Tasks left undone can even intrude into your dreams at night and, in extreme cases, lead to nightmares.

Avoiding procrastination takes some discipline. There are certain techniques, however, that can help:

• *Make a "to do" list for the day.* Then rank your list from most to least important. Start with the most important and work your way through. If unexpected circumstances limit what you can accomplish that day, you will have put your limited time and energy toward the most important tasks. And this will leave you with a sense of accomplishment.

• *Finish what you start.* Leaving

projects half done is sometimes worse than not starting them at all. An incomplete job will occupy your mind and make relaxing difficult. Also, work that is partly done robs you of the satisfaction that comes with closure.

• *Keep promises to do tasks on time.* Make schedules and stick with them. When promised work is late, it only becomes more difficult to face as time goes by.

• *Learn to say "no."* Sometimes we procrastinate because we feel overwhelmed by all of our commitments. Still, we continue to volunteer for tasks or projects because we don't want to tell someone "no." To combat this habit, make an effort to look realistically at your schedule and responsibilities before you commit to optional activities, and realize that knowing when to say "no" is better for your sleep and your health than worrying about tasks you can't hope to accomplish.

5. Nap Sparingly

Some people swear by naps; others find that napping during the day disrupts their sleep at night. The urge to nap is greatest about eight hours after we awaken from a night's sleep. This is when our body temperature begins the first of two daily dips (the other, more dramatic dip, occurs at night). A short nap in the early to middle afternoon can bring a renewed sense of energy and alertness. A nap in the late afternoon or early evening, on the other hand, can disrupt your sleep cycle and make it difficult to fall asleep when you retire for the night.

To benefit most from a nap, take it no later than mid-afternoon and keep it under 30 minutes. If you nap for a longer period, your body lapses into a deeper phase of sleep, which can leave

you feeling groggy when you awaken. If you are severely sleep-deprived and can't go on without a nap, it is better to sleep for a longer time to allow yourself to go through one complete sleep cycle. An average sleep cycle takes about 90 minutes in most people.

If you find you need a nap every day, take it at the same time so your body can develop a rhythm that incorporates the nap. It's also possible to use naps to temper the negative effects of an anticipated sleep deficit. For instance, if you know you are going to be up late because of special plans, take a prolonged nap of two to three hours earlier in the day. This has been shown to reduce fatigue at the normal bedtime and improve alertness, although it may throw off your normal sleep rhythm temporarily.

6. Eat and Drink Wisely

How much of a direct effect diet has on sleep is still unclear. It's safe to say, though, that a balanced, varied diet full of fresh fruits, vegetables, whole grains, and low-fat protein sources can help your body function optimally and help ward off chronic conditions such as heart disease. And since chronic diseases and the drugs required for them can interfere with sleep, eating wisely can help you safeguard your health and your sleep.

Adjusting your eating routine may also help you get a better night's sleep. Most people in this country eat a light breakfast, a moderate lunch, and a large meal in the evening. Yet leaving the largest meal to the end of the day may not be the best choice, since it can result in uncomfortable distention and possibly heartburn when you retire for the night. You might want to try reversing that pattern for a more sleep-friendly meal plan:

- Eat a substantial breakfast. Because you are breaking your nighttime fast and consuming the nutrients you will need for energy throughout the morning, breakfast should be your largest meal of the day. Whole-grain breads and cereals, yogurt, and fruit are just a few examples of good breakfast choices.

- Opt for a moderate lunch. Choose brown rice, pasta, or whole-grain bread and a serving of protein—fish, eggs, chicken, meat, or beans.

- Finish with a light dinner. It is particularly important to eat lightly for your evening meal in order to prepare for a good night's sleep. Plan to finish your meal at least two hours before going to bed, preferably longer. If you need a little something to eat before you hit the sack, you'll find suggestions for late night snacks a bit later in this chapter.

In addition, you may want to try these tips:

- Reduce or eliminate caffeine, especially in the late afternoon and evening. Caffeine is a stimulant, which is why so many of us reach for that cup of coffee in the morning to get us going. And it's true that some individuals can drink caffeinated beverages all day long and still sleep soundly at night. But if you're having trouble sleeping, then limiting your caffeine intake should be one of the first steps you try to help improve your sleep. Be aware that coffee is not the only source of caffeine. Many sodas and teas, chocolate, and some medications, especially those for headaches, also contain caffeine. Check labels to help eliminate such sources of stimulation.

- Some people are sensitive to the flavor enhancer and preservative monosodium glutamate (MSG). In susceptible individuals, it can cause digestive upset, headaches, and other reactions that can interfere with sleep. MSG is found in some processed foods and in some Asian foods. Try avoiding foods that contain MSG to see if it helps you sleep better.

- Drink the majority of your fluids for the day by the end of dinner. A full bladder may be cutting into your sleep time. Drink plenty of water throughout the day. Water is essential to healthy bodily functions. Shoot for eight glasses, or two quarts, per day. But be sure to drink the majority of your fluids before dinnertime so you won't be making numerous trips to the bathroom during your sleeping hours. Skip the alcohol. Despite making you feel drowsy, alcohol may actually be disturbing your sleep.

Schedule Your Sleep

It might seem unnatural to schedule your sleep like you would an important appointment, but this is one of the most vital principles to getting a good night's rest. Most of us begin our day with a morning routine. It helps us prepare ourselves physically and mentally for the day. So why not establish a bedtime routine that helps to prepare you for sleep? The purpose of a bedtime ritual is to send a signal to your body and mind that it's time to sleep. You probably already have some regular bedtime habits, even if you haven't realized it. Brushing and flossing your teeth, lowering the thermostat, and setting your alarm clock may all be part of your evening routine. To help you get to sleep, you should perform these activities in the same manner and order every night.

Establishing some type of bedtime ritual also provides closure to your day and allows you to go to bed and sleep with a more quiet body and mind.

Some people think going to bed on a schedule is only for children. While it's good for children to have a regular bedtime, it's also very good for adults who want to sleep like children when they hit the sack.

This regularity helps set your internal sleep-wake clock.

Within weeks of keeping a regular sleep-wake schedule, you will begin to feel more alert than if you were keeping a variable sleep/wake routine. Not only will a stable rhythm of sleeping and waking improve the quality of your sleep, but it will probably also improve the quality of your life. Try it for six weeks to gauge the difference it makes in your energy and alertness.

Ease into Sleep

Now that you know how to prepare for sleep during the day and schedule it at night, you're ready for bed. But before you peel those sheets back, consider how you might prepare your body and mind for that relaxing and peaceful sleep for which you long. The hour before bedtime is the most critical for good sleep. When used properly, the time right before bed can help you let go of the stressful, anxiety-provoking events of the day. But if that last hour before slumber is not used properly, it can set the stage for a long night of tossing and turning. Try some of the following ideas to see which work best for you.

1. Seek Serenity

The key to preparing for sleep is to establish an atmosphere of peace and calm. Ease your mind and body with quiet yet pleasurable activities. You will create a sense of inner well-being that allows sleep to come quickly and easily.

- Read to relax. But choose your reading material with care. The idea is to read something light that won't stimulate your mind. In other words, you probably don't want to crack that new software manual. Better choices would be a popular magazine, a short story, or perhaps devotional reading.

- Listen to music. Choose music that relaxes you. In general, soft instrumental music has the most calming effect. Hard driving rock and pop beats often pull you into the music, causing you to be more awake, especially if the tunes are familiar. Another sound alternative might be playing a recording of nature sounds.

- Try meditation or prayer. These activities, which help many people relax, can also help you be at peace with whatever is on your mind.

- Watch television, but only if it helps you relax. Watching television is fine if you use some discipline. Falling asleep with the TV on is not the best way to start your sleep. In most cases, you have to awaken to turn it off, which forces you to have to fall asleep again. The idea is to stay asleep once you doze off. A better use of television is to watch it earlier in the evening and practice other relaxation techniques right before bed. If you must watch right before bed, don't watch in your bedroom.

2. Take a Warm Bath

One popular way to relax the body and slow down the mind is a warm bath, and you may find it fits the bill for you. But you may want to do some experimenting with your timing. Some people find a nice hot bath just before bed makes them drowsy and ready to drop into sleep. On the other hand, some people find that a hot bath is actually stimulating or that it makes them too uncomfortably warm when they slip into bed. If you find a just-before-bed bath makes it harder for you to fall asleep, consider taking the bath earlier, a couple of hours before bed. An earlier bath may enhance the gradual drop in body temperature that normally occurs at night and help trigger drowsiness.

3. Let It Go

You've just gotten off the phone with a relative who infuriates you every time you talk with them. Flying into your bedroom like a whirlwind, you try to get ready for bed. You lie down on the bed and repeatedly slam your fist into your pillow as you try to find a comfortable position. But you can't fall asleep. Too often people go to bed when their mind is a raging fury, agonizing over some event of the day. When your emotions are boiling over, stay out of the bed and the bedroom until you cool down. Try journaling or writing your frustrations down on paper to help unburden your mind.

4. Make Your Bed a Haven

Most of us think of our bed as a place to sleep. But many people also use their bed for watching television, listening to the radio, talking on the telephone, eating, reading, or playing cards. If you really want to do all you can to sleep better, however, you shouldn't do any of these non-sleep activities in bed. When you do, the bed and bedroom can become associated with these activities rather than with sleep. Instead, you want to condition your mind and body to become drowsy and ready for sleep when you get into your bed, not ready and alert for a chat with a friend or a drama on TV. If you're one of those folks who sets the timer on the television or radio and drifts off listening to it, you might want to break yourself of the habit. You may not realize it, but you may be fighting off sleep just to hear the end of that monologue or the last bars of that favorite song. In addition, if you condition yourself to fall asleep only when you have that background noise, then if you wake up in the middle of the night, you may not be able to fall asleep without it. So you either struggle to fall back asleep without it or wake yourself up just to turn the device back on—neither of which is likely to improve your sleep overall.

5. Stop Trying
While lying in bed, tossing and turning, you may become frustrated at your inability to slip into slumber. The more you try to will yourself into sleep, the more conscious you become of not being able to doze off.

But sleep is unlike most activities in life. While trying harder is often the surest path to success in business, sports, or other waking activities, it is the surest path to failure when you want to sleep. Sleep is most easily achieved in an atmosphere of total relaxation. Your mind should be empty of thought or turned to soothing and calming thoughts. Your body should be relaxed, your muscles free of tension. If you find you can't fall asleep, the best solution is to get out of bed. That's right. Contrary to popular belief, the solution is not to stay in bed. If this happens with any frequency, and you do stay in bed, you may begin to associate your room and bed with feeling frustrated, uncomfortable, and unhappy. When you walk into your room, you'll immediately begin to worry about how long it will take to fall asleep.

> ### Hide the Alarm Clock
>
> *The bedside clock can be your number one enemy when you're having difficulty falling asleep. It acts as a constant reminder of how long it is taking to fall asleep. So rather than letting it stare you in the face all night, set it for the waking time desired, then hide it away from your reach, or at least turn it around so you can't see the time.*

Let your body associate any feelings of wakefulness with some other part of your home. Go to the kitchen for a drink of water. Go into another room and read, sew, or draw. Almost any activity will do as long as it's calming, relaxing, and doesn't require intense concentration. Gradually, you'll become tired and bored. Usually, within 15 to 20 minutes, your body will be ready for you to try to sleep again.

6. Snack Lightly Before Bed

If hunger pangs strike as you're preparing for bed, have a light snack. Research indicates that a light snack can help you sleep more soundly. The emphasis, of course, is on light. Bedtime is no time to stuff yourself. An overly full belly can be just as detrimental to sleep as an empty one.

Some researchers emphasize the importance of eating

a nighttime snack that is high in carbohydrates, such as bread, potatoes, cereal, or juice. The carbohydrates, they contend, help usher tryptophan into the brain, where it is converted into serotonin. Some sleep scientists recommend eating foods that are rich in magnesium and/or calcium. These minerals have a calming effect on the nervous system, and even a slight deficiency of them, they say, can affect sleep. Dairy foods are good sources of calcium. Sources of magnesium include fruits such as apples, apricots, avocados, bananas, and peaches; nuts; and whole-grain breads and cereals. You might want to experiment with snacks from these various groups to see if they help you sleep.

7. Actively Relax

An excellent way to quiet your body and mind before bedtime is to use one of the active relaxation techniques. These techniques help you to deliberately clear your mind of intrusive thoughts, wring the tension from your body, and put yourself into a peaceful state.

- Try progressive muscle relaxation (PMR). When you tense a muscle for a few seconds, it naturally wants to relax. That is how PMR works. You start at your toes and deliberately tense one muscle group at a time, progressively working your way up the body. To prepare, lie on your back on the floor or on a couch or recliner in a room other than your bedroom. Begin by scrunching your toes as hard as you can for ten seconds, while keeping the rest of your body relaxed. Then relax your toes, and tighten and release your calf muscles, again leaving your other muscles relaxed. Continue through the other muscle groups. Take your time at it; performing the muscle relaxation one time, from toes to head, should take at least 20 minutes. You should feel very relaxed when you finish. If you don't, repeat the entire cycle one more time.

• Try abdominal breathing. Rhythmic breathing is one of the best ways to help your body relax. There are many variations. This particular technique appears simple, but you'll need a little practice to do it properly. First, lie down on your back and begin to breathe normally. Now place your hand on your lower abdomen, just at your belt line, and slowly fill your lungs with air to the point that you can feel this portion of your abdomen rise. Take in as much air as you can and hold it for a couple of seconds. Then slowly release all the air in your lungs. Try to pay attention to nothing but the slow intake and release of air, the rhythmic rising and falling of your abdomen; don't rush. Repeat this eight to ten times.

• Try visualization. Imagine your favorite vacation spot. Maybe it's sitting on the sand with your bare feet being massaged by the ocean surf, or scuba diving off some coral reef. Alternately, think of an activity you find especially relaxing: drawing, cooking, hiking, walking your dog, even shopping. The idea behind visualization is to use your imagination to envision something that tells your mind to enjoy itself instead of being focused on some worry or concern.

Protect Your Head

Any discussion of the ways in which you can preserve youthful cognitive functioning as the years go by would not be complete without emphasizing the importance of shielding your brain from head injury and potentially toxic substances. Such assaults can cause lasting physical and cognitive damage.

Head Injury

If you want to make sure that your mind stays as sharp as possible for as long as possible, it's essential that you do all you can to avoid injury to your head. A growing body of research links head injury—especially the kind that causes traumatic brain injury (TBI)—to lasting and sometimes devastating problems with cognition, memory, and other brain functions. It is also linked to a higher risk of Alzheimer's disease and other forms of dementia. So it simply makes sense to protect your head.

Awareness of the potential dangers of head injury has been growing in the United States. That increased attention is likely due at least in part to the expanding population of older Americans, who have an increased incidence of falls, as well as to the much-publicized struggles of several retired professional athletes who suffered traumatic brain injury from repeated head blows during their playing days.

Even a mild bump on the head can send the brain crashing into the bony cranium, disrupting normal brain function and causing TBI. TBI may be the result of direct physical damage to the brain as well as of a brief lack of oxygen flow to the brain cells, which prompts swelling inside the skull. Even what appears to be a very mild head injury can cause swirling movements throughout the brain, tearing nerve fibers and causing widespread blood vessel damage. Bleeding in the brain may cause even more damage. The temporal lobes of the brain appear to be especially sensitive to this kind of injury, so sensory and motor-control issues often accompany the cognitive, behavioral, and emotional problems that can result from TBI.

Heads Up!

Traumatic brain injuries sent more than 2.2 million people to the emergency room, hospitalized more than 280,000, and contributed to the deaths of more than 50,000 in 2010.

TBIs can range from mild to severe, depending on whether unconsciousness occurred and for how long; the severity of the symptoms caused by the TBI is also taken into account. A mild TBI, the kind that occurs most often, is commonly called a concussion and is not considered life-threatening. Loss of consciousness may not occur, but if it does, it lasts for no more than 30 minutes. Symptoms of a mild TBI can include confusion, dizziness, blurry vision, headache, ringing in the ears, nausea and vomiting, talking incoherently, changes in sleep or emotions, difficulty remembering new information, and an inability to remember what happened immediately before, during, and after the injury. Such symptoms may begin right after the injury or may only develop hours, days, or even weeks afterward, and they can last for months or even years.

A moderate TBI is one that causes loss of consciousness that lasts from 30 minutes to 24 hours, and a severe TBI causes unconsciousness lasting more than 24 hours. The symptoms of moderate and severe TBIs are similar to those of a mild one but their severity is increased. Both can be life-threatening. And both moderate and severe TBIs—as well as repeated blows to the head—can lead to a heightened chance of developing Alzheimer's disease and other types of dementia.

Among the top causes of TBIs are motor-vehicle accidents and falls. The best way to protect your head—and the rest of your body—from serious injury in a motor-vehicle crash is to wear your seat belt every time you are in a moving vehicle, no matter which seat you occupy or how short the trip.

Falls are the leading cause of TBIs, and they hit older individuals especially hard. More than 80 percent of TBIs in adults aged 65 and older are the result of falls. Falls also prompt the most hospitalizations for TBI in people 45 years of age and older.

Aging can take a toll on eyesight, mobility, balance, and reaction time, increasing the risk of falls. To help keep you on your feet, try the following steps:

- Have your vision checked. If you're nearsighted, make sure your corrective lenses are up to date, and be sure to wear them. You have to be able to see obstacles in order to avoid them.
- Strengthen your legs with

regular exercise. The leg muscles can grow weaker with age and leave you more vulnerable to falls.

- Avoid drinking alcohol. It affects balance, slows reflexes, and can leave you dizzy or sleepy.
- Review your medications with your doctor or pharmacist. Many over-the-counter and prescription medications can cause dizziness or light-headedness. Sleeping pills and heart and blood pressure drugs are among them. Taking multiple medications can aggravate the problem.
- Get rid of clutter in your home, especially on stairs, in hallways, and near doorways. It just creates obstacles for you to trip over.
- Wear well-fitting, low-heeled shoes with rubber soles both indoors and out. Stockings, socks, and slippers don't provide enough traction and can even make you more likely to slip. You might also want to skip open-backed shoes, which can slide off your feet as you're climbing stairs.
- Replace throw rugs that don't have skid-proof backs; if you can't, then make sure they are tacked down.
- Make sure every staircase has sturdy handrails and is well lit. Never try to go up or down stairs in the dark; even in the middle of the night, turn on the lights.
- Make sure the rooms and hall-ways in your home are well-lit. Install more powerful bulbs or add lamps if necessary.
- Keep a flashlight next to your bed, and check it every so often to make sure it's in working order.

- Use nonstick mats in all tubs and showers, and install grab bars near the tub, shower, and toilet; consider getting a raised toilet seat.
- Purchase a cordless phone that comes with multiple handsets and distribute the handsets around your home (or at least in the most-used areas, such as the kitchen and bedroom), so you don't have to race across your home when the phone rings.
- Spread salt or even cat litter on icy walkways, stairs, porches, and driveways. And make sure these areas outside your home are well-lit at night; consider having motion-controlled fixtures installed.

Ride Right

To help protect your brain, always wear a helmet when riding a bicycle. Ask the salesperson at your local bike shop to help you get an appropriate fit. And be sure to keep the straps snapped and properly tightened during the entire ride.

Toxins

All your efforts to protect your brain from external blows will be for naught if you make lifestyle choices that assault your brain from within. And that's exactly what you're doing if you smoke cigarettes, abuse alcohol, or use illegal drugs. These toxins can stunt your brain's ability to withstand the passage of time.

Cigarette Smoking

If you're a smoker, puffing on that cigarette may make you feel reenergized—for a moment. But smoking can actually lower the amount of oxygen that reaches your brain, thereby affecting its functions, including memory and cognition. In fact, studies have found that smokers score lower on memory tests than do nonsmokers, and smokers who average more than a pack a day have an especially difficult time recalling names and faces. Some studies suggest that smoking can slow your recall ability about as much as having a couple of drinks. Smoking a pack a day exposes you to a variety of noxious substances, including 1,000 micrograms of toluene, which is highly toxic and can cause confusion and memory loss (as well as other damage). In other words, if you want to prevent premature brain (and body) aging, kick the habit. These days there are all sorts of products and programs that can help. Contact your doctor or local hospital to find out more.

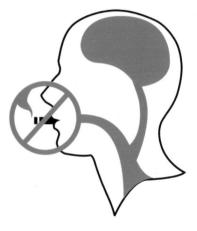

Alcohol Abuse

Regularly having a few beers or glasses of wine (or a few of any alcoholic beverage) can begin to interfere with your brain function. Alcohol abuse destroys brain tissue and interferes with the process of absorbing information so that it never enters long-term memory. Indeed, short-term memory loss is often the first sign that alcohol-related neurological damage has occurred; it's also a hallmark of alcoholism. This type of memory loss means a person has difficulty remembering new information, so the learning process takes

longer. Alcohol abuse also reduces higher-level thinking, or the ability to think in abstract terms, which is important for sound decision making, planning, and other abilities. If untreated, chronic alcohol abusers may even develop a form of dementia marked by disorientation, confused thinking, and severe amnesia. To put it plainly, excessive drinking actually changes the underlying brain chemistry that controls our abilities and skills. It can, and often does, threaten jobs and relationships. And it can certainly age your brain before its time. If you are struggling with alcohol, help is available. Contact your doctor or hospital for information about local programs and resources.

Out of It

People who habitually drink too much may experience blackouts—periods of amnesia that occur when the amount of alcohol consumed prevents the formation of memories in the brain. Having a blackout is not the same as passing out. Indeed, they are not always marked by visibly altered states of consciousness. For example, a person may go out for drinks with friends and talk about work but then the very next morning not be able to recall that any such conversation even took place. How long blackouts last varies from person to person. But having them for any length of time is considered an early high-risk indicator of alcoholism.

Recreational Drugs

When it comes to keeping your brain in tip-top shape no matter your age, there's no upside to dabbling in recreational drugs. The risk of lasting damage to your thinking and memory is simply too great. Marijuana, for example, can cause immediate as well as ongoing problems with short-term memory and attention. And both short-term and long-term use of opiates can negatively impact recall, reflexes, attention, concentration, hand-eye coordination, and executive functions. Recreational-drug use can even trigger symptoms that are similar to those of dementia.

Prescription Drug Caution

Some prescription medications can cause memory and cognitive problems. To avoid or minimize such effects:

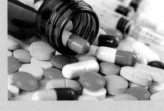

- *Show your doctor a list of everything you take, including prescription and over-the-counter medications, vitamins and minerals, supplements, and herbs.*
- *Fill all of your prescriptions at the same drugstore, so that the pharmacist can spot potential drug interactions, including those that can cause memory or cognitive problems.*
- *Never combine medications (even over-the-counter ones) with alcohol.*
- *Take your medicines exactly as prescribed. Never double a dose without your doctor's approval, even if you missed the previous dose.*

Focus on Remembering

Have you ever walked out of a mall and completely forgotten where you parked your car? If it happened to you when you were 20 years old, you probably didn't think anything of it. Once you're in your fifties and sixties, however, you may begin to wonder if such memory gaps are due to aging—or something worse.

But no matter your age, occasionally forgetting where you parked your car or where you left personal items is often completely normal. It's known as "everyday forgetting," and it's so common because it involves things we do every day and usually don't spend much time paying attention to. And that lack of attention is the very reason these instances of everyday forgetting occur.

Of course, as you get older, you're more likely to think— and worry—about memory problems. And the more you worry about them, the more likely you are to notice each and every slip. Odds are you forgot quite a few things when you were in your teens and twenties, but you never paid much attention to those lapses, and you certainly didn't worry about them. The fact is, the more you expect to have memory problems, the more you'll notice them.

The best way to stop this vicious circle is to focus on remembering instead of forgetting. Rather than expending mental energy fretting about every little memory slip, you need to pay more attention to the act of remembering. Once you begin to do this, you'll be amazed at how much better your memory will be.

Remember How Memory Works

Your baby's first cry . . . the taste of your grandmother's molasses cookies . . . the scent of an ocean breeze. These are memories that make up the ongoing experience of your life. They're what make you feel

comfortable with familiar people and surroundings, tie your past with your present, and provide a framework for the future. In a profound way, it is our collective set of memories—our "memory" as a whole—that makes us who we are.

Most people talk about memory as if it were a thing they have, like bad eyes or a good head of hair. But your memory doesn't exist in the way a part of your body exists—it's not a "thing" you can touch. It's a concept that refers to the process of remembering. In the past, many experts were fond of describing memory as a sort of tiny filing cabinet full of individual memory folders in which information is stored away. Others likened memory to a neural supercomputer wedged under the human scalp. But today, experts believe that memory is far more complex and elusive than that—and that it is located not in one particular place in the brain but is instead a brain-wide process.

Do you remember what you had for breakfast this morning? If the image of a big plate of fried eggs and bacon popped into your mind, you didn't dredge it up from some out-of-the-way neural alleyway. Instead, that memory was the result of an incredibly complex constructive power—one that each of us possesses—that reassembled disparate memory impressions from a web-like pattern of cells scattered throughout the brain. Your "memory" is really made up of a group of systems that each plays a different role in creating, storing, and recalling your memories. When the brain processes information normally, all of these different systems work together perfectly to provide cohesive thought.

What seems to be a single memory is actually a complex construction. If you think of an object—say, a pen—your brain retrieves the object's name, its shape, its function, perhaps even the sound when it scratches across the page. Each part of the memory of what a "pen" is comes from a different region of the brain. The entire image of "pen" is actively reconstructed by the brain from many different areas. Neurologists are only beginning to understand how the parts are reassembled into a coherent whole.

If you're riding a bike, the memory of how to operate the bike comes from one set of brain cells; the memory of how to get from here to the end of the block comes from another; the memory of biking safety rules from another; and that nervous feeling you get when a car veers dangerously close, from still another. Yet you're never aware that these are separate mental experiences nor that they're coming from all different parts of your brain, because they all work together so well. In fact, experts tell us there is no firm distinction between how you remember and how you think.

This doesn't mean that scientists have figured out exactly how the system works. They still don't fully understand exactly how you remember or what occurs during recall. The search for how the brain organizes memories and where those memories are acquired and stored has been a never-ending quest among brain researchers for decades. Still, there is enough information to make some educated guesses. The process of memory begins with encoding, then proceeds to storage and, eventually, retrieval.

Encoding

Encoding is the first step in creating a memory. It's a biological phenomenon, rooted in the senses, that begins with perception. Consider, for example, the memory of the first person you ever fell in love with. When you met that person, your visual system likely registered physical features, such as the color of their eyes and hair. Your auditory system may have picked up the sound of their laugh. You probably noticed the scent of their perfume or cologne. You may even have felt the touch of their hand. Each of these separate sensations traveled to the part of your brain called the hippocampus, which integrated these perceptions as they were occurring into one single experience—your experience of that specific person. Experts believe that the hippocampus, along with the frontal cortex, is responsible for analyzing these various sensory inputs and deciding if they're worth remembering. If they are, they may become part of your long-term memory. As indicated earlier, these various bits of information are then stored in different parts of the brain. How these bits and pieces are later identified and retrieved to form a cohesive memory, however, is not yet known.

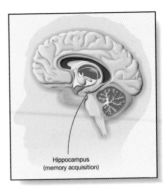

Hippocampus
(memory acquisition)

Although a memory begins with perception, it is encoded and stored by nerve cells using the language of electricity and chemicals. The connections between nerve cells in the brain aren't set in concrete—they change all the time. Brain cells work together in a network, organizing themselves into groups that specialize in different kinds of information processing. As one brain cell sends signals to another, the synapse between the two gets stronger. The more signals sent between them, the stronger the connection grows. Thus, with each new experience, your brain slightly rewires its physical structure. In fact, how you use your brain helps determine how your brain is organized. It is this plasticity that can help your brain rewire itself if it is ever damaged.

As you learn and experience the world and changes occur at the synapses and dendrites, more connections in your brain are created. The brain organizes and reorganizes itself in response to your experiences, forming memories triggered by the effects of outside input prompted by experience, education, or training.

These changes are reinforced with use, so that as you learn and practice new information, intricate circuits of knowledge and memory are built in the brain. If you play a piece of music over and over, for example, the repeated firing of certain cells in a certain order in your brain makes it easier to repeat this firing later on. The result: You get better at playing the music. You can play it faster, with fewer mistakes. Practice it long enough and you will play it perfectly. Yet if you stop practicing for several weeks and then try to play the piece, you may notice that the result is no longer perfect. Your brain has already begun to forget what you once knew so well.

To properly encode a memory, you must first be paying attention. Since you cannot pay attention to everything all the time, most of what you encounter every day is simply filtered out, and only a few stimuli pass into your conscious awareness. If you remembered every single thing that you noticed, your memory would be full before you even left the house in the morning. What scientists aren't sure about is whether stimuli are screened out during the sensory input stage or only after the brain processes its significance. What we do know is that how you pay attention to information may be the most important factor in how much of it you actually remember.

Easier Encoding

If you want to remember a word, thinking about how it sounds or its meaning will help. Likewise, if you use visual imagery to help memorize something—such as meeting a person named Mr. Bell and thinking of a bell when you shake hands—you're more likely to remember it. Some experts believe that using imagery helps you remember because it provides a second kind of memory encoding, and two codes are better than one.

Memory Storage

Once a memory is created, it must be stored (no matter how briefly). Many experts think there are three ways we store memories: first in the sensory stage; then in short-term memory; and ultimately, for some memories, in long-term memory. Because there is no need for us to maintain

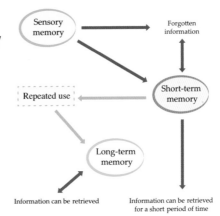

everything in our brain, the different stages of human memory function as a sort of filter that helps to protect us from the flood of information that we're confronted with on a daily basis.

The creation of a memory begins with its perception: The registration of information during perception occurs in the brief sensory stage that usually lasts only a fraction of a second. It's your sensory memory that allows a perception such as a visual pattern, a sound, or a touch to linger for a brief moment after the stimulation is over.

After that first flicker, the sensation is stored in short-term memory. Short-term memory has a fairly limited capacity; it can hold about seven items for no more than 20 or 30 seconds at a time. You may be able to increase this capacity somewhat by using various memory strategies. For example, a ten-digit number such as 8005840392 may be too much for your short-term memory to hold. But divided into chunks, as in a telephone number, 800-584-0392 may actually stay in your short-term memory long enough for you to dial the telephone. Likewise, by repeating the number to yourself, you can keep resetting the short-term memory clock.

Important information is gradually transferred from short-term memory into long-term memory. The more that you repeat or use the information, the more likely it is to eventually end up in long-term memory, or be "retained." (That's why studying helps people to perform better on tests.) Unlike sensory and short-term memory, which are limited and decay rapidly, long-term memory can store unlimited amounts of information indefinitely.

Types of Remembering

Psychologists have identified four types of remembering.

Recall: This is what you most often think of as "remembering" —the active, unaided remembering of something from the past.

Recollection: This is the reconstruction of events or facts on the basis of partial cues, which serve as reminders.

Recognition: This is the ability to correctly identify previously encountered stimuli—such as when you see your old teacher's face across the room and recognize who she is.

Relearning: This type of remembering is a testament to the power of the memory itself; material that's familiar to you is often easier to learn a second time.

People tend to more easily store material on subjects they already know, since the information has more meaning to them and can be mentally connected to related information that is already stored in their long-term memory. That's why someone who has an average memory may be able to remember a greater depth of information about one particular subject. Most people think of long-term memory when they think of "memory" itself—but most experts believe information must first pass through sensory and short-term memory before it can be stored as a long-term memory.

Memory Retrieval

When you want to remember something, you retrieve the information on an unconscious level, bringing it into your conscious mind at will. While most people think they have either a "bad" or a "good" memory, in fact, most people are fairly good at remembering some types of things and not so good at remembering others. If you do have trouble remembering something—assuming you don't have a physical disease—it's usually not the fault of your entire memory system but an inefficient component of one part of your memory system.

Let's look at how you remember where you put your eyeglasses. When you go to bed at night, you must register where you place your eyeglasses: You must pay attention while you set them on your bedside table. You must be aware of where you are putting them, or you won't be able to remember their location the following morning. Next, this information is retained, ready to be retrieved at a later time.

If the system is working properly, when you wake up in the morning you will remember exactly where you left your eyeglasses.

If you've forgotten where they are, you may not have registered clearly where you put them. Or you may not have retained what you registered. Or you may not be able to retrieve the memory accurately. Therefore, if you want to stop forgetting where you left your eyeglasses, you will have to work on making sure that all three stages of the remembering process are working properly.

If you've forgotten something, it may be because you didn't encode it very effectively, because you were distracted while encoding should have taken place, or because you're having trouble retrieving it. If you've "forgotten" where you put your eyeglasses, you may not have really forgotten at all— instead, the location may never have gotten into your memory in the first place.

Age Gap

Research suggests that older people have some trouble with all three stages of memory, but they have special problems with registering and retrieving information.

Distractions that occur while you're trying to remember something can really get in the way of encoding memories. If you're trying to read a business report in the middle of a busy airport, you may think you're remembering what you read, but you may not have effectively saved it in your memory.

Finally, you may forget because you're simply having

trouble retrieving the memory. If you've ever tried to remember something one time and couldn't, but then later you remember that same item, it could be that there was a mismatch between retrieval cues and the encoding of the information you were searching for.

Help Your Brain Play Fetch

You'll be better able to remember something if you use a "retrieval cue" that occurred when you first formed a memory. If you memorized a poem outdoors when birds were singing, then playing birdsong might help you recall the poem. This is why vivid memories will recur strongly when you experience a sensation that accompanied the

original event. It's why, for example, the sound of a car backfiring may trigger an unpleasant memory of a battlefield experience for someone who was previously in a war zone.

Signs of Something More

The following are common warning signs that memory problems may be more than everyday forgetfulness and therefore should warrant a medical evaluation:

- *Memory problems that affect job performance or interfere with everyday functioning*
- *Difficulties with language, such as frequently forgetting simple words or substituting inappropriate words*
- *Disorientation in familiar locales or in familiar situations*
- *Confusion about time of day, month, season, or decade*
- *Decreased or unusually poor judgment*
- *Memory problems accompanied by other symptoms such as extreme fatigue, loss of interest in activities that are typically enjoyed, rapid or unusual changes in mood, agitation, listlessness, problems with balance or coordination,*

headaches, vision problems, numbness, shortness of breath, or chest pain

It's important to keep in mind that there are a variety of factors that can cause memory problems, such as stress, vitamin deficiencies, and circulatory problems; not all memory problems signify the onset of Alzheimer's disease. That's why a thorough medical evaluation is needed when memory problems are out of the ordinary or prompt concern. Once the underlying cause is determined, it can often be treated, and the memory problems remedied as a result.

Pay Attention!

Everyday forgetting is linked to the fact that when you've done something so many times in the past, it can be hard to remember if on this particular day you've turned off the stove. Indeed, some people go through entire routines of "checking" in the morning because they know they have problems remembering if they've actually turned off appliances and closed windows before leaving for the day.

If you really want to cure such absentmindedness, you need to become acutely aware of what you're doing. When you don't pay attention, you're not likely to register information in the first place. The likely result: forgetting. Paying attention takes effort. There may be times when your attention strays—think of the times you've rushed out the door because you were running behind schedule, only to discover later that you left behind something important. Instead, you need to slow down and focus on one thing at a time.

It is important to concentrate on what you are doing,

especially when it comes to things you're not usually good at remembering. For example, have you ever been driving to work and tried to remember whether or not you unplugged the iron? To improve your ability to remember such everyday occurrences, you need to pause and pay attention as you turn off or unplug an appliance so that it will register in your memory. This helps to turn an automatic act into a conscious one.

Here are the steps:

1. Before going out the door, stop and take the time to think. If you're locking your back door, think about what you're doing.
2. Focus your concentration. Speak out loud to force yourself to pay attention. If you often forget to turn off the stove, go into the kitchen and force yourself to slowly survey the appliances. As you look at each one, say "The oven is turned off. The toaster is unplugged." When you're driving down the road and you ask yourself if the oven is off, you'll know that it is.
3. Go over everything. If you tend to leave important things behind, create a list of them, and line them all up before you leave. Go through each item, saying it out loud. Check your calendar to assure yourself that everything you need is lined up and ready.
4. Take immediate action. Do you need to take back that library book? Do it now, while you're thinking about it. At least put the book by the front door; lean it right up against the door if you have to.

If you're plagued with general absentmindedness, it could mean that your life is simply a bit out of control. You're most likely to be absentminded when you're preoccupied. Those who are easily distracted or who tend to be daydreamers are particularly vulnerable to interference.

Here's a quick list of ways to regain some control over your daily life and your memory:

1. Get organized. Develop a routine and stick to it. If you're organized, you can often make up for not remembering certain things by keeping information and various possessions in easily accessible places.

2. Make lists. Keep a daily to-do list, and cross off items once they've been done. Always keep the list in the same place, and organize the list into categories. Make your list easy to find: Put it on a large, colored sheet of paper.

3. Keep a calendar handy to keep track of important dates. Check the calendar at the same time every day so it becomes a habit. When you buy a new calendar at the beginning of the year, transfer all important dates from the old calendar.

4. Have a place for everything, and put everything in its place. If you have a key rack right inside your door, you'll be more likely to hang your keys there and remember where they are.

5. If you need to remember to take certain things to work or school, keep a tote bag or backpack right by the front door. Keep all papers and items that need to go with you in that bag or backpack.

6. Concentrate on one thing at a time, and try to pay active attention each time you put something down.

7. Make visual cues: Place a colored sticky note on your steering wheel, protruding up from your briefcase or purse, or on your bathroom mirror, your shoes, or your wallet. Don't assume you'll remember; leave reminders.

8. Keep important numbers in one place, so you can locate them even if you're under a lot of stress. Be sure to keep critical numbers (phone numbers, medical insurance, etc.) in your wallet.

9. Write things down as they occur—use lists, schedules, and so on. If you use a smart phone or tablet, type them into the device.

10. Return items that you frequently use to the same spot each time, and rely on placement to trigger your memory (for example, leave an umbrella on the doorknob).

11. Repeat yourself. If someone tells you information that you need to remember, repeat it over and over again to yourself.

12. Keep a positive attitude about memory lapses as

Think Positive

Even when memory lapses cause you some aggravation, try not to dwell on them. If you constantly tell yourself that you have a bad memory, it may become a self-fulfilling prophecy. Focus, instead, on how your memory is improving with the strategies in this book, and remember that nobody's memory is perfect.

you get older. Remember, memory decline is not inevitable. Be sensitive to the many things that can make you prone to forget. You can take action to overcome or mitigate most of them.

Work on Weak Spots

Not all aspects of memory slow down as we age. And whether young or old, some people are simply better at remembering certain things, like names, while other folks are good at recalling dates or directions. It is un-realistic to expect to remember everything. But you can get better at remembering those things that you aren't— and perhaps have never been—good at remembering. The following are strategies that you can employ to get better at remembering specific types of information.

Remembering Habitual Tasks

If you have trouble remembering habitual tasks such as turning off the coffee pot each morning or feeding the cat, the key to solving this problem is to relate the activity to something that you don't generally forget to do every day. For example, if you often  forget to take your medication in the morning, tell yourself each day that you won't eat your breakfast until you have taken your pill. Make swallowing that pill a prerequisite to taking your first bite of food. By incorporating a task into an outline of things that you don't forget to do, you will be less likely to forget that task. You can even make the connection a physical one, say by storing your bottle of medication right in front of your cereal box in the cabinet.

Recalling Where You Put Things

There is hope for those who can't remember where they left their car keys or their purse. The main reason you forget where you put these items is because you weren't paying attention when you put them down. Because you weren't paying attention in the first place, when it comes time to retrieve the memory of where you left the object, you can't. It was never properly absorbed into your short-term memory in the first place.

The solution is really quite simple: Pay attention. And if you can't pay attention, be consistent. Make a concerted effort to pay attention to where you are placing the keys. Stop yourself in the middle of dropping them on the desk and take a deep breath. Stare at the desk and say out loud, "I am putting my keys on the desk."

If you force yourself to pay attention, you're less likely to forget when it comes time to retrieve that particular memory. The other sure-fire way to

> **Memory Myth**
>
> *Myth: I just have a bad memory and there's nothing I can do about it.*
> *Fact: Remembering is a learned skill. It can be developed just like any other skill. In the absence of disease, the strength of your memory depends on how well you've mastered memory techniques. It's not a function of inborn memory ability.*

remember particular items is to put them back in exactly the same place, every single time. Find specific places to keep all the items that are often misplaced:

- Glasses
- Keys
- Medications
- Coupons
- TV remote
- Cell phone

Remembering Your Schedule

It won't matter much if you can remember to do something in the future if you don't remember to do it at the right time. For example, you may remember that you need to mail in your IRS payment a week before the deadline, but if you forget all about the task on the day you intended to do it and the deadline subsequently passes, you haven't solved your problem. In fact, a problem with remembering dates is one of the most common memory failures. A combination of mental strategies and mechanical reminders should help get this problem under control.

One way to solve the problem of forgetting dates is to cue your attention. For example, you could take your IRS payment and tape it to the front door, or tape a dollar bill to the front door to remind yourself. Here are some tried-and-true cues:

- Attach a safety pin to your sleeve.
- Put a rubber band around your wrist.
- Move your watch to the opposite arm.

- Leave a note to yourself (a brightly colored sticky note is ideal) in a prominent place.
- Set a reminder on your cell phone, tablet, or computer—but only if you use it every day.

Using a calendar is an excellent mechanical method of remembering dates. The key is not to use two calendars—one at home and one at work. Get one calendar that's convenient to carry with you. Or, if you  use a smart phone or can access your computer both at home and at work, try using the device's calendar program to keep track of appointments and important dates electronically. Whatever calendar you ultimately choose, all important days should be marked down. Every morning, consult the calendar and cross off items as they occur. On the first day of the new year, get out a new calendar and transfer all of the important dates from the old calendar so you don't forget anything.

Remembering What You're Doing

We've all gone into a room and totally forgotten what we're doing there. If you've done this, you're not alone; experts suggest that more than half of all Americans experience this problem. It's not incipient dementia; it's just a lack of attention.

Each time you have a thought about going into a room to get something, stop for a moment and tell yourself out loud what you are going to get. If you're already in the other room and can't remember what you're doing there, try retracing your steps to where you were standing when you had the thought to leave the room. This form of association will often help jog the memory of your errand.

Remembering Places

It's not unusual to forget where you've parked the car. Here's how to remember where you parked it: After you park your car in a big parking lot, don't just get out of the car and head straight for your destination. Stop. Look around and make a  mental note of where you are. Find something that will help you remember: Did you park next to a tall lamp post? Is there a parking number or letter posted to help you find your way? Check to see if there's a sign on the store or in the store window that aligns with the row you parked in, and repeat what the sign says to yourself as you enter the store. Better yet, write a description of the location on the parking garage ticket or other paper and put it with your keys. Don't rely on a description of the cars parked around you; they could very well be gone when you come back for your car.

If you tend to lose your way as you walk, ride your bike, or travel in a car, you need to better register the way as you go:

- As you travel, try to take mental snapshots along the route. Flash back to them in your mind once in a while.

- Record visual "cues" from both directions if you can (things might look different from the opposite direction). Look for that big red barn, the funny sign, the crooked tree.
- Use all your senses. Pay attention to unusual smells or noises; the more senses you involve, the stronger the memory trace will be.

Use GPS or maps. If your phone or car does not have GPS and you're not good at reading maps, write down directions, study them thoroughly before you leave, and bring them with you.

Make It Stand Out

If all else fails and you have a really hard time finding your car, try making it stand out: Attach a brightly patterned flag, a lightweight rubber toy (like a squeaky toy), or a neon table tennis ball to the tip of your car's antenna. This way, you'll

have a better shot at spotting your vehicle from a distance. You might also consider parking further out in the lot, where there tend to be fewer vehicles parked to begin with, so it's easier to pick out your car from a distance.

Remembering Quantities

If you've ever been in the midst of baking brownies and suddenly realized you have no idea how much flour you've dumped in the bowl, you need help in paying attention to amounts. Try visualizing the amount of flour in the measure. Pour it in while saying out loud the amount you're using, "One cup, two cups . . . " You'll find that when you comment out loud on how many cups you've put in, you're less likely to forget or get sidetracked.

You may want to resort to a backup strategy. For every cup of flour you pour, set aside an object to represent that cup: a coffee bean, a raisin, a spoon. Each time you add another cup of flour, set aside another bean or raisin. This way you can visually check exactly how much you've added, even if you're continually interrupted.

Remembering Names

There you are at a business party, chatting with someone whose name you've forgotten. A third person comes up and you're expected to make an introduction, but you can't remember the name.

This is certainly not unusual. Most of us can remember faces quite easily, even if we've only seen them once or twice. But when it comes to attaching a name to that face, that's another matter entirely. We tend to remember faces more readily because it involves the process of recognition, whereas attaching a name to the face requires a process called recall. What's the distinction? Recognition is much easier for the brain to accomplish, because recognition simply requires you to choose among a limited number of alternatives that are present in front of your eyes—sort of like a multiple-choice question. But to recall a name, the brain has to go digging for it, which is a much more complex process. Recall, then, is more like a fill-in-the-blank question.

Recall vs. Recognition

Trying to answer the following questions can help you understand the difference between recognition and recall.

Recall
Who was the president of the United States during the Civil War?

Recognition
Who was president of the United States during the Civil War?

> *A) Benjamin Franklin*
> *B) Abraham Lincoln*
> *C) John Quincy Adams*

The process of recall is generally easier if we have some retrieval cues that give the brain some direction. One way to do this is to associate an individual's name with another piece of information that you already

know. For example, when you first meet a person and hear their name, you might tell yourself that this person has the same name as your mother-in-law or the same name as your favorite baseball player.

You can also use the verbal technique to help implant a person's name in your memory when you first meet them. To do this, simply:

1. Register the person's name: Pay attention to it as it is said!
2. Repeat the person's name to yourself.
3. Comment on the name.
4. Use the person's name out loud as soon as possible.

Another strategy for remembering names is to use the visual technique. There are three simple steps to get the name right every time using this technique:

1. Associate the name with something meaningful. That's easy with a name like "Bales" (picture two bales of hay). If it's something more difficult, like Sokoloff, think of "Soak it all off" and picture a giant sponge sopping up spilled milk.
2. Note distinctive features of the person's face.
3. Form a visual association between the face and the name. If you've just met Jill Brown, and she has very dark eyes, picture those brown eyes as you say the name to yourself.

After you've done all you can to remember the name, you need to rehearse the name if you're going to remember it. Repeat the name to yourself again in about 15 seconds. If you've met several people, repeat the names to yourself while picturing the faces before the end of the event. The more often you can repeat the names early on, the more likely they will stick in your head. Remembering names can be an important social skill; we all like to think that other people remember us. The ability to remember names of even slight acquaintances is highly regarded.

The Name Game

Here's one way to practice remembering names. Cut out ten magazine photos, each showing a person's face. Enlist a partner, give that person five of the photos, and keep the remaining five photos for yourself. Write a name on each of your five photos (pick five random names—preferably not the names of your children or your five best friends), and ask your partner to do the same with their five photos. Now exchange photos, and practice trying to associate the name with something distinctive about the person's face. Wait about 15 minutes, then quiz each other on the names.

Supercharge Your Memory Skills

If you're interested in greatly sharpening your memory, there are more sophisticated methods called mnemonic strategies that have been proven to aid memory. Some of them are fairly complex and take practice to learn, but they do work.

Linking or Chaining

The most basic strategy for remembering is called the link method (or "chaining"), which is particularly good for memorizing short lists. It's a form of visualizing, but with this system you must link the items together by thinking of images that connect them.
Here's how it works:

1. First, form a visual image for each item on the list.
2. Associate the image for the first item with the image for the second, and then link the second with the third, and so on.
3. To recall the list, begin with the first item, and then proceed in order as each item leads to the next one.

When using the link system, don't try to associate every item with every other item on the list; just associate the items two at a time. While a grocery list does not necessarily have to be remembered in order (although it sometimes helps you to find things faster), let's use it as an example.

- Cabbage
- Orange juice
- Pickles
- Bread
- Potatoes

1. Form a visual association between the cabbage and the pickles. You might, for example, imagine a pickle trying to roll a giant head of cabbage up a steep hill.
2. Next, create a link between the pickles and the potatoes: Imagine one giant dill pickle in a bow tie and tails dancing with a potato dressed in an evening gown.
3. Then, link the potatoes with the orange juice, perhaps by imagining the potato in a jogging suit swigging down a frosty glass of orange juice.
4. Finally, tie the orange juice to the bread, say, by visualizing a slice of bread with a sail, battling waves in a vast sea of orange juice.

Why such zany visuals? Well, we tend to notice and more easily remember things that are out of the ordinary. When you're creating images, the more vivid they are, the more likely they will stick in your head. It's also important to use the first association that pops into your mind, since this, too, will make it easier for you to remember the same association when you are trying to recall the list.

Here's a bigger list of words to try to chain.

- Shoe
- Pencil
- Book
- Flower
- Piano
- Bird
- Dog
- Basketball
- Tree
- Bus
- Pizza
- Door

One problem with this strategy is that, while each link is associated with the one before it, you have to be able to remember the first item on your own. And if you have a really bad memory for lists, you may find that quite difficult to do. To solve this problem, you should cue the first item in some way, preferably in a way that is related to the purpose of the list. If you're trying to remember a grocery list, for example, link the first item with the front door of the store. Using our previous shopping list, you could imagine a big green cabbage handing out sales fliers at the front door of the grocery store or perhaps sitting in a grocery cart and waving at you.

If you have a really bad memory, it's still possible that if you forget one item on the linked list, it may drag the item that it's linked to into oblivion as well. In that case, the method of loci may be a better choice. The method of loci, discussed later in this chapter, has an advantage over the link method because all of the items are linked to a place rather than to each other.

On the other hand, one nice thing about the link system is that once you are good at using it to remember a few items, you can move on to remember 20 or 30 items. Don't think so? Take this test and find out:

1. Have a friend give you a list of 20 items (the words should be nouns, not verbs or adjectives, and they should be concrete objects rather than abstract concepts).
2. Write down the first word, and associate it visually with your partner (for example, if the first noun is "chair," imagine your partner balancing a chair on their nose).

3. As you write down each consecutive noun, create a mental image that links it to the previous noun in the list.

4. Then give the list back to your partner, and try to recall the list using the mental images you created. You are likely to be amazed at how many items you can remember.

The more you practice this linking system, the more efficient you'll become at creating mental links between words in a list and the better your memory for lists will become.

The Story System

A close cousin to the link method is the story system, in which you link the items you want to remember in a story. Using our previous grocery list, you could create a story like this:

The cabbage picked up a jar of pickles to throw at the potato, who slipped in a puddle of orange juice and landed on a mattress made of bread.

Link vs. Story

Scientists say that both methods can help you learn and remember lists of items. The link system can help you remember up to three times as many items as you could without it, while the story method is very effective if you're trying to remember concrete words. Both methods are more effective than either rehearsal or imagery alone.

You can see that the story system, unlike the link system, links all of the items in an integrated narrative. This can make it much easier for you to remember all of the items, since the items occur in a logical framework instead of in an unrelated association of pairs. On the other hand, it takes some time and creativity to weave together a story that incorporates all the items in a list. Some people simply aren't good at making up stories, and even those who are may find it difficult if the list has more than a few items, because the story becomes rather complex quite quickly. In addition, like the link system, the story system makes it difficult to recall items out of sequence.

Method of Loci

The oldest known mnemonic strategy is called the method of loci ("loci" is the plural of locus, which means location). It's based on the assumption that you can best remember places that you are familiar with, so if you can link something you need to remember with a place that you know very well, the location will serve as a clue that will help you to remember. Here's how it works:

1. Think of a place you know well, such as your own house.
2. Visualize a series of locations in the

place in logical order. For example, picture the path you normally take in your house to get from the front door to the back door. Begin at the front door, go through the hall, turn into the living room, proceed through the dining room and into the kitchen, and so on. As you enter each location, move logically and consistently in the same direction, from one side of the room to the other. Each piece of furniture could serve as an additional location.

3. Place each item that you want to remember at one of the locations.

4. When you want to remember the items, simply visualize your house and go through it room by room in your mind. Each item that you associated with a specific location in your house should spring to mind as you mentally make your way through your home.

Here's how it would work if you wanted to remember the following shopping list:

- Shaving cream
- Ketchup
- Peaches
- Ice cream
- Hot dogs

As you visualize your house, imagine spraying shaving cream all over the front door. Don't just imagine the word "shaving cream." Really see it as you depress the nozzle and spray the foam all over the front door. Try to imagine the smell of the shaving cream, as well.

Now open the door, enter the hall, and imagine a giant peach rolling down the steps in the front hall and heading right for you. Now walk into the living room, and visualize a six-foot-tall hot dog in a bun wearing a cowboy hat and lounging by the fireplace. Enter the dining room and picture a bottle of ketchup, dressed in an old-fashioned maid's uniform, setting the table. Finally, go to the kitchen and picture a gallon of ice cream, melting as it slaves over a hot stove.

After you've visually placed all your list items around the house, when you try to remember your shopping list, all you have to do is visualize your front door. You will instantly see the shaving cream; as you enter the hall, the peach will pop into your mind; and so on. The more outrageous and unusual you make your mental images, the easier you'll find it is to remember them. You can use this method to remember lists of items, important points in a speech, names of people at an event or meeting, things you need to do, even a thought you want to keep in mind. This method works well because it changes the way you remember, so that you use familiar locations to cue yourself about things. Because the locations are organized in an order that you know well, one memory flows into the next very easily.

You can adapt this system by adding other buildings you know very well: your office building, a mall, your friend's house, a trip through your town, your garden—any place you know well. It doesn't
matter how close or how far apart each room or location is. What is important is how distinct one place is from another. In other words, you might not want to use your town library, which is probably built with identical aisles of shelves filled with books. In addition to making each

location very distinct and memorable, you'll want to be sure to have an association between an item and its location by having the item and location interact. If you were trying to remember the First Amendment and visualized a reporter just standing beside a desk in the front hall, it would not be as memorable as it would be if the reporter were busy typing the Constitution at the desk in your front hall.

You can also place more than one item in any location. If you have a list of 50 grocery items to remember, you could place five items at each of ten locations. Each of these five items should interact at its location. For example, you might think of your daily routine, beginning at home:

- Your bedroom
- Your bathroom
- Your kitchen
- Your garage
- The driver's seat of your car

Now you must link the items that you want to remember to each of these places. Of course, first you must remember the places, but this should be easy, because they are a part of your daily routine. Then chain each item to a place; remember, the more creative and vivid your ideas, the better. Using the grocery-list example: You wake up next to a giant can of shaving cream; you find a giant peach having a bubble bath in your bathroom; a hot dog in a chef's hat is cooking you breakfast; a bottle of ketchup on wheels is parked in your spot in the garage; and a gallon of ice cream, wearing a seatbelt and sunglasses, is melting in the driver's seat. You could then picture five more items along your route to work, five more in your office, and so on.

Both the linking and the loci methods allow you to remember items on a list, but neither lets you locate just one particular item. For example, if you wanted to find the tenth item using the linking system, you'd have to work your way down through the first nine items to get to it. Of course, this is true for anything we learn in a serial way: Most people wouldn't be able to name the nineteenth letter of the alphabet without counting from A to S first.

The way around this problem is to place a distinguishing mark at every fifth place. Using the loci method, at the fifth place, you could incorporate a five-dollar bill into the image. At the tenth location, you could incorporate an image of a clock with its hands pointing to ten o'clock. The same thing can be done with the linking method: Incorporate a five-dollar bill image into the link between the fourth and sixth items, for example, or a ten-dollar bill between the ninth and eleventh. Using these added touches, there is really no limit to the number of things you can remember with either of these two methods.

Go Hog Wild!

With visual types of mnemonic strategies, such as linking and method of loci, you'll get the most bang for your memory buck if you create witty, goofy, or just plain unusual mental images. We just naturally tend to remember incidents, situations, and even personalities that are unexpected or that stand out from the crowd.

Peg Systems

Peg systems are probably the best known of all memory systems. In these systems, items to be remembered are pegged to, or associated with, certain images in a prearranged order. The idea behind the peg systems has been traced to the mid-1600s, when it was developed by Henry Herdson, who linked a digit with any one of several objects that resembled the number (for example, "1 candle"). The system gets its name from the fact that the peg words act as mental "pegs" on which you can hang the information that you need to remember.

The peg method is a better memory strategy than either the link or loci method because it's not dependent on retrieving items in sequence. You can access any item on the list without having to work your way through the whole thing. It is, however, a bit more complicated to learn at first. In the peg system, you learn a standard set of peg words, and then you link the items you need to remember with the pegs. The peg method can be used to remember ideas and concepts and to organize activities as well as to remember lists for shopping and errands.

The various forms of the peg system all use a concrete object to represent each number. What is different is how you choose the object that represents each number. One peg system relies on using pegs that look like the

Worth the Work

The various peg systems may take a bit more time and effort to learn than the linking or method of loci systems, but once you've mastered a peg system, you'll be amazed at how much you're able to recall.

numbers they represent, another relies on pegs that rhyme with the number, one relies on meaning, and another uses alphabetic pegs. Two of the easiest peg systems to master are the rhyming and alphabet forms, which we'll discuss here.

Rhyming Pegs (Visual Pegs)

The best-known of the peg systems is the rhyming peg method, in which numbers from one to ten are associated with rhymes: one-bun, two-shoe, and so on. This system was introduced in England around 1879 by John Sambrook. The system is easy to use, and many people already know many of the standard rhymes from the nursery rhyme "one, two, buckle my shoe." In order to use the system, you must memorize the words that rhyme with numbers one through ten (most peg systems don't include a peg word for zero, but you can make one up yourself):

1 = bun	2 = shoe	3 = tree
4 = door	5 = hive	6 = sticks
7 = heaven	8 = gate	9 = vine
10 = hen		

1. Now, as you say each rhyme, visualize the item that the peg word represents. Picture it vividly—is the bun a hot dog bun or a hot cross bun? Is the shoe an old battered sneaker or a black high-heeled pump?
2. Now draw the item. The act of drawing will help you remember the rhyme, creating a strong mental

association between the numbers and the words that rhyme with them.

3. Imagine each peg word as vividly as possible. By visualizing the object that each word represents, you'll fix it securely in your mind, creating a strong mental association between the number and the word that rhymes with it.

Once you've formed an association between the numbers and the words that rhyme with them, you've constructed your pegs. Practice by saying each of the peg words out loud. Then try picturing the peg words in place of the numbers as you randomly jump amongst the numbers: five, three, one, eight. Because the words rhyme with the numbers, you don't have to say the numbers to remember the words.

If you want to remember a list, all you have to do is link each item with a peg: the first item with a bun, the second item with a shoe, and so on. To remember the list, call up each peg, and you'll automatically remember the mental image that is linked to each peg.

Here's how it could work for a short grocery list of milk, bread, eggs, and ham. You could start out by visualizing a jug of milk balancing a bun on its lid. Then imagine a muddy sneaker squashing a loaf of French bread. Then think of a tree filled with eggs. And finally, picture a ham in a beret banging on a door to be let in. When you get to the store and you think of one—bun—you'll think of a bottle of milk. Two—shoe—you'll see a shoe squashing the bread.

Peg words can help you remember lists of items or

errands and daily activities. This system may not work for those with memory problems caused by brain damage on one side of the brain, however, since it requires remembering in two distinct stages, one involving the right hemisphere and the other involving the left.

Alphabet Peg Systems

The alphabet makes a good system, since it is naturally ordered and everyone knows it. In order to create concrete images for the letters, each image either rhymes with the letter of the alphabet it represents or has the letter as the initial sound of the word. The alphabet peg system might be: A = hay, B = bee, C = sea. Peg words can be created that rhyme with or sound similar to the letters of the alphabet that they represent:

A = hay	B = bee	C = sea
D = deep	E = eve	F = effect
G = geology	H = age	I = eye
J = jay	K = quay	L = elm
M = Emma	N = end	O = open
P = pea	Q = cue	R = art
S = essay	T = tea	U = you
V = veer	W = double you	X = exit
Y = why	Z = zebra	

If you don't like the rhyming aspect of the alphabetic peg-word system, you can come up with a list that doesn't rhyme but that simply uses the same letter of the alphabet to begin each word.

A = artichoke	B = bat	C = cake
D = dog	E = elephant	F = fireman
G = goat	H = horse	I = iron
J = jelly	K = kangaroo	L = llama
M = mouse	N = napkin	O = orange
P = pail	Q = queen	R = rat
S = shoe	T = tank	U = umbrella
V = vase	W = wagon	X = xylophone
Y = yarn	Z = zebra	

The only problem with using the alphabet system is that most people don't automatically know the numeric equivalent of the alphabet, so things can't be directly retrieved as easily. For example, most people don't know, without counting, that S is the nineteenth letter, so if they wanted to recall the nineteenth item out of sequence, they would have to count off the letters and then retrieve the associated image.

Other Peg Systems

You can also select peg words on the basis of meaning: one = me (there is only one "me"); three = pitchfork (three prongs); five = hand (five fingers on a hand). Numbers make good peg words because they have a natural order, and everyone knows them. Unfortunately, this system is limited because it's hard to find good peg words to represent numbers beyond ten.

Chunking

One good way of remembering information is to use chunking; that is, grouping separate bits of information into larger chunks in order to better remember them. Often, organizing them in a particular way, such as according to sound, rules of grammar, or rhythm can help you recall them. For example, if you want to remember a ten-digit phone number (9991357920), it's much easier to break it up into chunks of two, three, and four digits: 999-135-7920. That's why social security numbers are given in chunks of three, two, and four (999-99-9999) instead of as one unbroken number (999999999). Remembering things is easier when the information is grouped in smaller chunks.

Acrostics

An acrostic is a phrase that uses the first letter of a word as a cue to remembering it. If you were a young medical student, one of the most familiar acrostics you would use would be: On Old Olympus' Towering Top A Famous Vocal German Viewed Some Hops.

What does this mean? The first letters of each of the words in this phrase stand for the first letter of each of the cranial nerves, in order: olfactory nerve (1), optic nerve (2), oculomotor nerve (3), trochlear nerve (4), trigeminal nerve (5), abducens nerve (6), facial nerve (7), vestibulocochlear nerve (8), glossopharyngeal nerve (9), vagus nerve (10), spinal accessory nerve (11), and hypoglossal nerve (12).

And if you want to remember the order of the colors in a rainbow, just remember the name Roy G. Biv. Each letter in his name stands for a color: R= red; O = orange; Y = yellow; G = green; B = blue; I = indigo; V = violet.

An Acrostic Quiz

Can you tell what objects either of these acrostics represents?

My Very Early Morning Jog Starts Up North

My Very Excellent Mom Just Served Us Nachos

The first letter of the words in each phrase represent the planets, in order, starting closest to the Sun: Mercury, Venus, Earth, Mars, Jupiter, Saturn, Uranus, Neptune

---

Using Mnemonics to Remember Speeches

There you are at your desk, staring down at five pages of a speech that you're supposed to give to your colleagues tomorrow evening. You're struggling to memorize every last word but you're worried that, come tomorrow, your memory will fail you. What should you do?

Contrary to what you might think, you should not try to memorize the speech word for word. A memorized speech doesn't sound like a spontaneous, off-the- cuff set of remarks—it sounds canned and therefore can be rather boring and flat. Even Jay Leno would probably put viewers to sleep if he recited a memorized speech.

What's worse, if you do try to memorize a speech and you forget a word or phrase, odds are you'll panic, and that will only compound your memory problems.

Of course, you can sidestep this problem by reading your speech right from the paper, but that's worse than memorizing it—it's a sure way to lose your audience. And woe to you if you lose your place—more fumbling and panic.

Ideally, what you want to do is to appear before your audience and calmly have a conversation with them, in your own words, explaining what you want to say. Sound impossible? Not at all. The best speakers do this every day, using the same techniques that you can master. There is a whole range of mnemonic strategies you can use to help you remember a speech without having to learn the whole thing word for word and without reading it from cue cards or index cards. What's a speech, anyway, but a series of thoughts strung together in an interesting way? If you can use your own words and follow a logical sequence, you'll be home free.

To do this, you'll have to write out the whole speech, to make sure you cover the important points. Next, you can simply choose one of the mnemonic techniques we discussed above. One of the oldest ways of remembering a speech is to use the method of loci, in which you place information in imaginary locations. To remember the information, you remember the location. Here's how to remember a speech using this method:

1. Write down the main points of your speech.
2. Choose a familiar building to place the main points of your speech: Your own home is a good choice.
3. Visualize the first point of your speech at your front door.
4. Visualize the second point of your speech in your hallway.
5. Move through your home in a logical sequence, leaving one main point in each room.
6. When you stand up to give your speech, simply go to your front door: The main point will be waiting for you. Mentally work your way around the rooms, and you'll cover all the main points of your speech.

Visualize It!

When you have something that you need to remember, "see" it in your mind. You need to create a mental picture of it, and as mentioned previously, the more unusual or absurd you make the image, the more likely you are to remember it. For example, if you go to the mall and park the car on level C in the space that's marked number five, you might imagine that there are five chickens waiting in your car for your return. The "chickens" stand for level "C" of the garage, and the fact that there are five of them tells you that your car is in space number five.

Of course, the loci system isn't the only way to remember a speech. You can use a different mnemonic strategy if you prefer. Some people prefer the linking system for remembering the key points in a speech. They select a key word to represent a whole thought, and they link each of the representative words together.

Study Tips

Kara doesn't much like American history, and she's put off studying for the final exam on Friday. On Thursday night, she stays up and reads over each chapter from beginning to end. But when she sits down to take the test the next day, she can't seem to remember a thing that she read. What happened?

Kara went about studying for the test in the wrong way. Simply sitting down the night before and reading through the entire chapter, without questioning, commenting, or categorizing, with the vague hope that she'd remember what she read, is pretty much like throwing a batch of file cards into a box and hoping to remember what's on them later.

Unfortunately, Kara's study methods are pretty common among students. Studying for a test just by reading over the information one time will give you a retention rate of only about 20 percent, no matter how smart you are.

Fortunately, by learning some simple retention strategies, you can boost your recall to more than 80 percent. Memory strategies can help you learn spelling, vocabulary, a foreign language, names of historical figures, states and capitals, scientific terms, cities and primary products, U.S. presidents, foreign kings, basic math—just about everything a person needs to learn in school or on the job.

There are three main ways to boost your memory of basic facts:

1. Practice active recall during learning.
2. Periodically review the material.
3. Overlearn the material beyond the point of bare mastery.

Involve Yourself in Reading

Instead of just reading, you need to read and think about what you're reading. Here are some suggestions for doing just that:

Think of questions for yourself before, during, and after the reading session.
- Ask yourself what is happening next, why it's happening, and what would happen if one event or fact was different.
- Note what interests you. Take a moment to make a mental comment out loud.
- Train yourself to summarize, a section at a time. What are the main points in the text you just read? What are the logical conclusions?

Visualize as You Read

Try to imagine yourself in the place you're reading about, or try to imagine yourself doing what you're studying. Include yourself in images that you build in your mind. If you're reading about the Civil War, picture yourself on the battlefield. Why are you there? What is the enemy doing, and why? The better you can put yourself into a scene, the better you'll remember what you are reading.

Of course, it's much easier to visualize yourself in a battle than it is to link yourself to the major exports of Peru. Instead of just trying to visualize "wool, wheat, and corn," imagine you're a Peruvian farmer raising sheep and growing wheat and corn. This will work with just about anything, except perhaps for numbers and dates.

Be There!

It's generally easier to learn and retain new concepts if we have hands-on experience with them. For example, you're more likely to remember how to change a tire if you've actually changed one before. You can put a similar strategy at work when you're learning about a different time period or different country: Try to really visualize yourself being in the middle of the action. The more you can imagine yourself as being part of the story, the more likely you'll be to grasp and retain the gist of the information.

Take Note!

Taking notes won't help you if you scribble down the words in class without thinking about what you're writing, which is unfortunately the way too many students take notes. Try this:

1. Take them carefully while thinking about their content.
2. Review them as you write.
3. Summarize whenever possible. Isolate what's

important and discard the rest while
you're writing.

4. Don't take down every word your teacher says.

Use PQRST

One of the most popular techniques for remembering
written material is the PQRST method: Preview,
Question, Read, State, and Test. Memory experts think
this works better than simple rehearsal because it
provides you with better retrieval cues.

Preview. Skim through the material briefly. Read the
preface, table of contents, and chapter summaries.
Preview a chapter by studying the outline and skimming
the chapter (especially headings, photographs, and
charts). The object is to get an overview of the book or
chapter (this shouldn't take more than a few minutes).

Question. Ask important questions about the
information you're reading. If the chapter includes
review questions at the end, read them before you begin
reading the chapter and try to keep them in mind as you
go. What are the main points in the text? How does the
action occur? Read over the paragraph headings and ask
yourself questions about them.

Read. Now read the material completely, without taking
notes. Underlining text can help you remember the
information, provided you do it properly. The first time
you read a chapter, don't underline anything (it's hard
to pick out the main points the first time through). Most
people tend to underline way too many things, which
isn't helpful when you want to be able to go back later

and review important points. Instead, read over one section and then go back and, as you work your way through each paragraph, underline the important points. Think about the points you're underlining.

State. State the answers to key questions out loud. Reread the chapter and ask yourself questions and answer them out loud. Read what you've underlined out loud, and think about what you're saying. You should spend about half your studying time stating information out loud.

Test. Test yourself to make sure you remembered the information. Go through the chapter again and ask questions. Space out your self-testing so you're doing it during a study session, after a study session, and right before a test. If you'd like, enlist the help of a friend to quiz you.

Make the Most of Studying

When you study is almost as important as how you study. It's better to schedule several shorter study sessions rather than one marathon all-nighter. This is probably because you can only concentrate for a certain period of time. If you try to study in one long session, you won't be able to maintain your concentration throughout. Breaks help you consolidate what you've learned.

On the other hand, you can overdo the short sessions as well. The trick is to determine the optimum length of a study session and how many sessions work best for you and for the material. Research suggests that difficult information or inexperienced students require shorter sessions for best results. If you have several subjects to study, it's better to separate them and spread them out over several days. You should also vary your learning methods: Take notes one day, make an outline the next, recite information out loud during the third study session.

You'll also want to avoid interference when you study. Study, then go to bed, so nothing else can interfere with what you've learned. Studies have also shown that sleeping between studying and testing is the best way to do well on a test. A person who sleeps right after studying will remember more than someone who stays awake.

It's also true that other activities between studying and the test will influence how well you remember. If you've spent several hours studying French, you shouldn't then study Latin before going to bed. In fact, if you have two very similar subjects to study, it's best not to study them in the same location.

Try First-Letter Cueing (Acronyms)

The use of the first letter of a word as a cue to remembering the word itself can be helpful in remembering material. This cueing usually employs acronyms—making a word out of the first letters of the words to be remembered. For example, it's possible to remember the Great Lakes using the acronym HOMES (Huron, Ontario, Michigan, Erie, Superior).

Another related type of first-letter cueing is the acrostic, discussed previously, in which the first letters in a series of words form a word or phrase. For example, names of the strings of the viola (CGDA) can be remembered by the acrostic: Cats Go Down Alleys.

Because the acronym system is so effective, most organizations and governmental bodies make use of first-letter cueing: NATO (North Atlantic Treaty Organization) or AA (Alcoholics Anonymous). Some acronyms are so well known that the original full name has been all but forgotten, as in "scuba" (Self-Contained Underwater Breathing Apparatus) gear.

The only problem with first-letter cueing is the propensity to forget what the strategy has been used for. Therefore, it's a good idea to make the association remind you  of the information to be remembered. Imagine HOMES floating on the Great Lakes, so that when you want to think of the names of all the lakes, the image of HOMES will return to you and with it, the first letter of each of the lakes.

Give Peg or Link a Shot

Both the peg and linking systems that we discussed earlier in this chapter also work well with studying school subjects. Review those methods and try practicing with them, especially for rote learning and memorization (such as a list of U.S. Presidents or the amendments to the Constitution).

Exercise Your Mind

You can improve your mind at any age. And many experts agree that one of the best ways to keep your mind sharp—or improve it if it's starting to show some signs of age—is to exercise it throughout your life.

We've all heard that getting regular physical activity can keep your heart muscle strong and flexible. And we explored how physically moving your body's muscles can help protect your brain. Well, even though your mind is not a muscle, it, too, needs regular mental exercise to perform the way it should year after year. One great way to exercise your mind and keep it nimble is to continually stimulate it with new and interesting experiences and opportunities to learn. Another is to challenge it with a wide range of puzzles, riddles, games, and activities that allow it to stretch its proverbial legs and run. These forms of mental calisthenics will prompt the creation and activation of more connections between nerve cells as well as the birth of new nerve cells in cognitively important areas of

the brain. The more numerous and active your brain-cell connections and the faster they become at sending signals back and forth, the better your mind will work.

Stimulating a Better Brain

Modern neuroscience has established that our brain is a far more elastic organ than was previously thought. In the past it was believed that an adult brain could only lose nerve cells (neurons) and couldn't acquire new ones. Today we know that new neurons—and new connections between neurons—continue to develop throughout life, even well into advanced age. Thanks to recent scientific discoveries, we also know that we can harness the powers of plasticity to protect and even enhance our minds at every stage of life—including our advanced years. Recent scientific research demonstrates that the brain responds to mental stimulation much like muscles respond to physical exercise. In other words, you have to give your brain a workout. The more vigorous and diverse your mental life the more you will stimulate the growth of new neurons and new connections between neurons. Furthermore, the *nature* of your mental activities influences *where* in the brain this growth takes place. The brain is a very complex organ with different parts in charge of different mental functions. Thus, different cognitive challenges exercise different components of the brain.

Thanks to MRI and other sophisticated imaging technologies, we know that certain parts of the brain grow in size in people who use these parts of the brain more than most people do. For example, in one study, researchers found that the hippocampus, a major player in spatial memory, was larger than usual in London cab drivers who were required to remember and navigate complex routes in the huge city. Other studies have revealed that Heschl's gyrus, a part of the brain's temporal lobe that is involved in processing music, is larger in professional musicians than in musically untrained individuals. And the angular gyrus, the part of the brain involved in language, proved to be larger in bilingual people than in those who speak only one language.

What is particularly important about these findings is that the size of the effect—the extent to which the part of the brain was enlarged—was directly related to the *amount of time* each person spent in the activities that rely on the part of the brain in question. For instance, the hippocampal size was directly related to the number of years the cab driver spent on the job, and the size of Heschl's gyrus was associated with the amount of time a musician devoted to practicing a musical instrument. Enlargement of a brain region indicates a greater than usual number of neurons and synapses. What these research findings show, therefore, is that our behavior directly influences and changes the structure of the brain. The impact of cognitive activity on the brain can actually be great enough to result in an actual increase in its size!

It is also true that any more or less complex cognitive function—be it memory, attention, perception, decision making, or problem solving—relies on a whole network of brain regions rather than on a single region. Therefore, any relatively complex mental challenge will engage more than one part of the brain, yet no single mental activity will engage the whole brain.

For this reason, it is important to have a rich, challenging, and diverse mental life. The more vigorous and varied your cognitive activities, the more efficiently and effectively they'll protect your mind from decline. To return to the workout analogy: Imagine a physical gym. No single exercise machine will make you physically fit. Instead, you need a balanced and diverse workout regimen. The same is true for your brain.

Expand Your Mind's Horizons

As long as you stay active, interested in life, and engaged in the world around you, your memory and other cognitive abilities don't have to deteriorate as you grow older. Research shows that enriching your surroundings, your daily experiences, and your life as a whole can pay off in a sharper, more resilient mind.

For example, animal studies have found that rats living in cages with plenty of exciting toys and lots of stimulation have larger, healthier brain cells and a larger outer brain layer. Deprived rats living in barren cages, on the other hand, have smaller brains.

Research in humans strongly indicates that stimulating the brain in a variety of ways throughout life can help to protect cognitive function. It also appears to provide a kind of mental reserve that helps delay signs of normal brain aging as well as loss of cognitive function related to Alzheimer's disease and other types of dementia.

What can you do to enrich your brain's environment? Get out and see new places, meet new people, and experience new things. For example:

• Take up a new hobby or sport.

- Visit museums, art galleries, or historical sites in your area that you've never previously taken time to explore.
- Take a class at a community college, or go back to school and get the degree you've always wanted.
- Check out listings for free lectures or seminars at your local library, civic center, or senior center, and attend those that pique your interest.
- Join a volunteer organization or a book club.
- Investigate your ancestors and plot out your family tree.
- Track down old friends and find out what's been happening in their lives since you last communicated.
- Make sure you have music playing for at least a little while every day; while any music is good, research has found that classical music is especially stimulating to the intellect.
- Keep lots of books on hand, and make time to read them. If you can't block out specific reading times, keep a paperback in your purse or briefcase or download a book to your tablet or e-reader so you can squeeze in some reading while you're riding a train or bus or waiting for an appointment.
- Add a fish tank to your home or office with lots of colorful fish and interesting tank toys.
- Paint the walls of your home interesting, unusual colors. Select interesting art, knickknacks, rugs, and curtains. Try to include a variety of textures with things like pillows, blankets, and furniture fabrics.

- If you have the space, put a birdhouse and a bird feeder or birdbath outside your window, and keep a pair of binoculars handy. Add some brightly colored flowers to your yard or place planters or window boxes outside your windows.
- Don't forget the flowers indoors, too; the colors and smells will be an added sensory boost.
- Set out a jigsaw puzzle or chessboard and regularly engage visitors in a game.
- Plug in a computer and use it to surf the Internet or play a challenging game; computer games can improve memory in such fun ways you'll hardly notice the effort.
- Try cooking food from a different culture, or visit restaurants with cuisines that are not usually on your menu.
- Include others in your life. Some research indicates that strong social connections can help stave off depression and Alzheimer's disease and keep you alert and interested in life. Make an effort to spend time with other people, especially if you do not have relatives or close friends nearby. Get to know your neighbors by inviting them over for a cup of coffee or glass of lemonade. Attend some of the various get-togethers held at your house of worship so you can meet other congregants. Keep an eye out for interesting social activities and gatherings or volunteer opportunities in your area and use them as ways to meet potential new friends.

Remember, anything that engages the senses will help to stimulate your mind and strengthen your memory. So touch, feel, smell, and experience new things as often as you can.

Picture This!

Visualization is another good exercise for your brain. Try to visualize something from your childhood: your bedroom in the house where you grew up, your first-grade classroom, the inside of your parents' car when you were a teenager. Visualization helps stimulate the mind and exercise the brain cells. If you picture a happy or comforting place from your past, visualization can also serve as a relaxation tool by giving you a pleasant mental detour away from worries.

Play Games with Your Mind

As we've learned, there is no single magic pill to protect or enhance your mind, but vigorous, regular, and diverse mental activity is the closest thing to it. Research indicates that people engaged in mental activities as a result of education or vocation are less likely to develop dementia as they age. In fact, many of these people demonstrate impressive mental alertness well into their eighties and nineties.

The important thing is to have fun while doing something good for yourself. Puzzles, like the ones in this book, can be engaging, absorbing, and even addicting. An increasing number of people make regular physical exercise part of their daily routines and miss it when circumstances prevent them from exercising. These habitual gym-goers know that strenuous effort is something to look forward to, not to avoid. Similarly, you will strengthen your mental muscle by actively challenging it. Don't put a puzzle down when the solution is not immediately apparent. By testing your mind you will discover the joy of a particular kind of accomplishment: watching your mental powers grow.

You must have the feeling of mental effort and exertion in order to exercise your brain.

This brings us to the next issue. While all puzzles are good for you, the degree of their effectiveness as brain conditioners is not the same. Some puzzles only test your knowledge of facts. Such puzzles may be enjoyable and useful to a degree, but they're not as useful in conditioning your brain as the puzzles that require you to transform and manipulate information or do something with it by logic, multistep inference, mental rotation, planning, and so on. The latter puzzles are more likely to give you the feeling of mental exertion, and they are also better for your brain health. You can use this feeling as a useful assessment of a puzzle's effectiveness as a brain conditioner.

Try to select puzzles in a way that complements, rather than duplicates, your job-related activities. If your profession involves dealing with words (e.g., an English teacher), try to emphasize spatial puzzles. If you are an engineer dealing with diagrams, focus on word puzzles. If your job is relatively devoid of mental challenges of any kind, mix several types of puzzles in equal proportions.

Cognitive decline frequently sets in with aging. It often affects certain kinds of memory and certain aspects of attention and decision making. So it is particularly important to introduce cognitive exercise into your lifestyle as you age to counteract any possible cognitive decline. But cognitive exercise is also important for the young and the middle-aged. We live in a world that depends increasingly on brain power. It is important to be sharp in order to get ahead in your career and to remain at the top of your game.

How frequently should you exercise your mind and for how long? Think in terms of an ongoing lifestyle change and not just a short-term commitment. Regularity is key, perhaps a few times a week for 30 to 45 minutes at a time. Research shows that even a relatively brief regimen of vigorous cognitive activity often produces perceptible and lasting effects. But as with physical exercise, the results are best when cognitive exercise becomes a lifelong habit.

Anywhere Word Addition

Here's a little brain-stimulating word activity you can play even when you're standing in line at the grocery store or waiting for a doctor's appointment.

Think of a noun: horse, for example. Now add a verb to form a short sentence, such as "The horse ran." Now try to substitute new verbs for "ran," such as "the horse bucked," "the horse jumped," and "the horse whinnied." Once you run out of verbs, add an adjective to each noun-verb combo: "the black horse ran," "the wild horse jumped," and "the frightened horse whinnied," for example. Keep building more and more complex and varied sentences. Before you know it, your wait time will be over, but you'll have spent it sharpening your thinking skills.

The Final Lap

Now that you've taken the time to learn about different factors that affect your brain age, let's complete a final assessment to see how far you've come. An overly easy puzzle will not stimulate your brain, just as a leisurely walk in the park is not an efficient way to condition your heart. You need mental exertion!

To that end, we've tried to find the "challenge zone" to give you insight into your strengths relative to where you began *Lower Your Brain Age*. These puzzles are similar in difficulty to those in the first assessment. You will use many of the same cognitive skills and you will feel more assured as you complete these puzzles.

Research has shown the benefits to our brains of following challenging mental regimens. Fortunately, you can engage in activities that are both good for your brain and fun—one such activity is working puzzles. We hope that the assessments in this book will give you a sampling of how fun it can be to train your brain.

As with the first assessment, set a timer for 60 minutes to complete these 12 challenging puzzles. Work through them at your own pace but notice that you feel more confident in your ability to complete them and do well.

SOLVE IT

Solve each problem in your head, then circle the correct answer.

40 × 4 =	160 260 360	
33 ÷ 3 =	9 11 30	
60 + 81 =	131 141 151	
96-51 =	45 46 48	
130 ÷ 2 =	40 60 65	
55 ÷ 55 =	0 1 55	
14 × 14 =	176 186 196	
78 + 32 =	98 110 112	

53 − 24 =	19 28 29	
153 ÷ 3 =	51 57 150	
140 ÷ 4 =	20 35 40	
100 − 42 =	48 52 58	
20 + 31 =	41 45 51	
11 × 13 =	131 133 143	
40 ÷ 4 =	10 20 44	

Answers on page 191.

CAN YOU FIND IT?

Ignoring spaces and punctuation, how many occurrences of the consecutive letters F-I-N-D can you find in the paragraph below? Circle each instance.

Jeff indicated he found a lot of stuff in Dallas when he left Flint indiscreetly to work as a pathfinder with the deaf Indian he met while searching for some kind of indigo-colored staff in desolate corners of town. A refined fisherman who felt stiff indoors, Jeff fried a fish he caught and had the fin delivered to a friend in Flint, a buff inductee in the Finnish air force named Findley. Finding himself in dire need of funds, Findley sold the fin despite warnings from Jeff indicating it would put his life in disarray.

Answers on page 191.

AROUND THREE CUBES

Each group of cubes has one line that wraps around it. Determine which two cubes have lines that make the exact same pattern.

CHANGE IN THE AIR

How fast can you arrange the stacks of coins from smallest to largest in monetary value? Write the letter order in the blanks.

___ ___ ___ ___ ___ ___

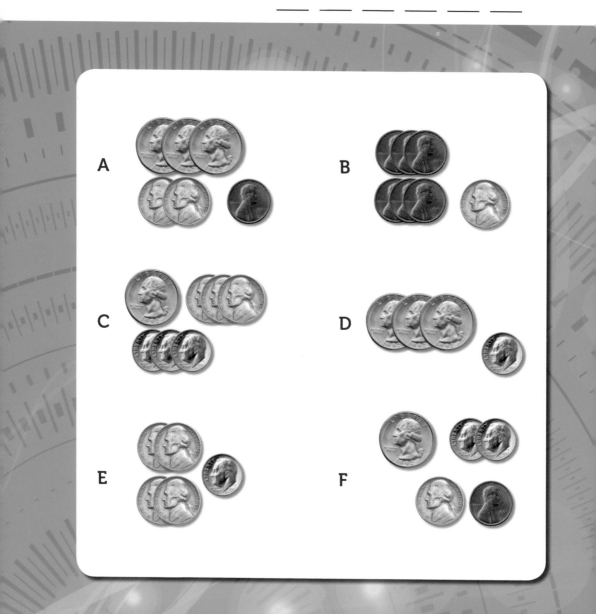

Answer on page 191.

REMEMBER ME

Look at the pictures for 2 minutes. After 2 minutes, turn the page.

REMEMBER ME

Which objects did you see? Circle Yes or No next to each object's name.

Cow	YES NO	Ponytail	YES NO
Easel	YES NO	Tomahawk	YES NO
Calculator	YES NO	Haystack	YES NO
Tool belt	YES NO	Whale	YES NO
Molar	YES NO	Ears of corn	YES NO
Football	YES NO	Backpack	YES NO

Answers on page 191.

THE ANSWER MAN

· ·

Read the story that follows. Then turn the page for a quiz on what you've read.

Invictus Sigafoos was writing a book. Not just any book, mind you. This was *The Book of Answers*. It would be a guaranteed bestseller, he assured his friends, because it would have all the answers. "Got a question?" he said to his pal Eddie Shrdlu. "The answer is in the book."

"Come on, Vic," said Eddie. "Any question?"

"You got it, pal. Go ahead, ask a question."

"Okay. What can go up a chimney down but not down a chimney up?"

"That's on page 3," said Vic. "An umbrella."

"All right," said Eddie. "Pretty good. Here's another one: What is the one 11-letter word that all Harvard graduates spell incorrectly?"

"Page 17," said Vic. " 'Incorrectly.' "

"I'm impressed!" said Eddie. "So if you know everything, tell me this: What is the meaning of life?"

"Everyone knows that," said Vic. "42."

"Page 42?"

"No, just 42. Didn't you read *The Hitchhiker's Guide to the Galaxy*?"

The book was published and became a bestseller, just as Invictus had predicted. On his book tour, he arrived in Milwaukee and went to the hotel he was supposed to be staying at—only to find there wasn't a room to be had. The place was sold out!

"But I have a reservation!" said Invictus.

"I'm sorry, sir," said the desk clerk. "Some people have extended their stays. We don't have a single room."

Invictus needed an answer, but this one wasn't in his book. He had to think fast. He was the Answer Man!

"So," he said to the desk clerk. "If the President of the United States was in town and needed a place to stay, are you telling me you wouldn't get him a room?"

"Well," said the desk clerk. "If it was the President, I'm sure we would find him a room somehow."

"Great!" said Invictus. "I'll take his room! He's not coming."

THE ANSWER MAN

Circle an answer to each question.

1. What is Vic's full name?
   a) Invictus Sigafoos
   b) Invictus Shrdlu
   c) Incictos Answrdu

2. What was the name of the book Eddie wrote?
   a) *The Book of Answers*
   b) *The Book of Questions*
   c) none of the above

3. What is the answer to Eddie's first question?
   a) Incorrectly
   b) an umbrella
   c) 42

4. What page is the answer to Eddie's first question found on?
   a) 3
   b) 17
   c) 42

5. What city is named as being on the book tour?
   a) Madison
   b) Milwaukee
   c) Minneapolis

6. Eddie talks about the graduates of one college. Which college was it?
   a) Dartmouth
   b) Harvard
   c) Yale

7. Which book answers "42" to the question "What is the meaning of life?"
   a) *The Hitchhiker's Guide to the Galaxy*
   b) *The Meaning of Life*
   c) *Waiting for Godot*

8. What reason does the hotel clerk give for denying Invictus a room?
   a) The owner oversold the rooms.
   b) The hotel is closing for renovations.
   c) Some people extended their stays.

Answers on page 191.

BOOKEND LETTERS

Each word below is missing a pair of identical letters. Add the same letter to the beginning and end of each word to create new words. Do not use any pair of letters twice.

__earl__

__eat__

__elude__

__eve__

__evolve__

__euro__

A B C D E F G
H I J K L M
N O P Q R S T
U V W X Y Z

Answers on page 192.

LET'S GET COOKING!

How many dots can you find in the picture below? Circle the answer.

110 111 112 113 114

Answer on page 192.

AROUND FIVE CUBES

Three lines wind around five-cube groups as shown in the illustration. Each line is closed in a loop. Two of these have exactly the same pattern. They are not mirrored. Circle those two groups.

Answer on page 192.

MISSING SIGNS

For each equation, one sign will complete both sides of the equation. Fill in the blanks.

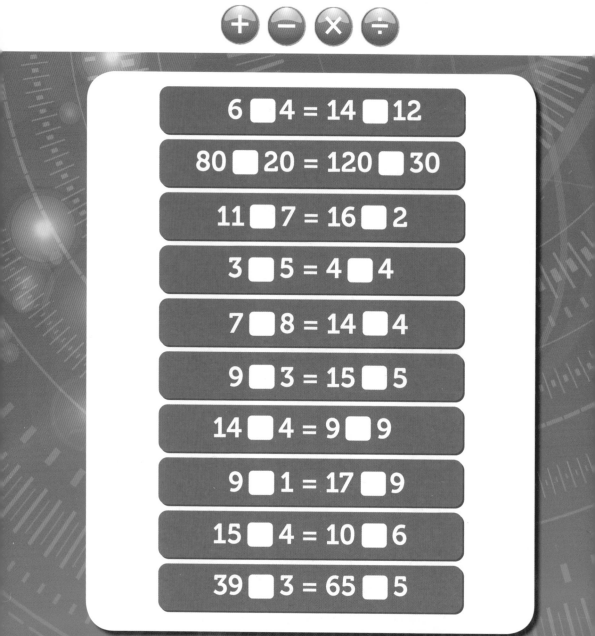

6 ☐ 4 = 14 ☐ 12

80 ☐ 20 = 120 ☐ 30

11 ☐ 7 = 16 ☐ 2

3 ☐ 5 = 4 ☐ 4

7 ☐ 8 = 14 ☐ 4

9 ☐ 3 = 15 ☐ 5

14 ☐ 4 = 9 ☐ 9

9 ☐ 1 = 17 ☐ 9

15 ☐ 4 = 10 ☐ 6

39 ☐ 3 = 65 ☐ 5

Answers on page 192.

WORD SQUARE AND MEMORY CHECK

Look at the word square for 2 minutes. After 2 minutes, turn the page.

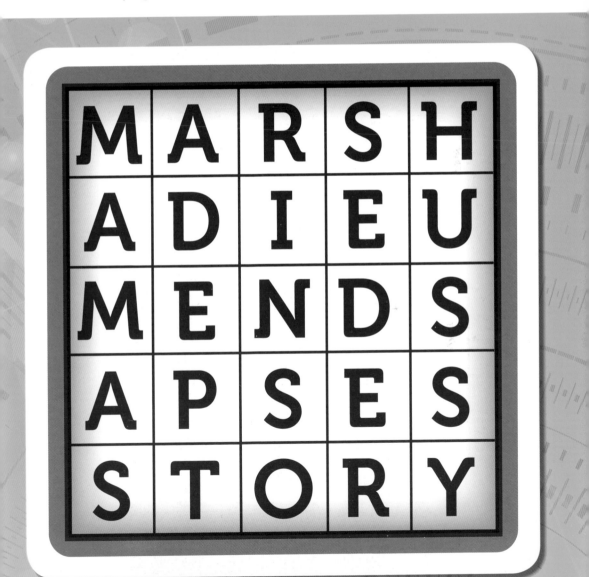

M	A	R	S	H
A	D	I	E	U
M	E	N	D	S
A	P	S	E	S
S	T	O	R	Y

WORD SQUARE AND MEMORY CHECK

Which words were part of the word square?

MINDS	YES NO	INEPT	YES NO
LENDS	YES NO	RINSO	YES NO
ADIEU	YES NO	SEVER	YES NO
FUSSY	YES NO	PAPAS	YES NO
STORY	YES NO	MAMAS	YES NO
GLORY	YES NO	HISSY	YES NO
HUSSY	YES NO	APSES	YES NO

Answers on page 192.

PATTERN MEMORIZATION

Look at the shapes for 2 minutes. After 2 minutes, turn the page.

PATTERN MEMORIZATION

What shapes complete the pattern? Fill in the blanks.

Answer on page 192.